D E V E L O P M E N T
I N   P R A C T I C E

Population
and
Development

Population
and
Development

Implications
for the
World Bank

THE WORLD BANK

WASHINGTON, D.C.

© 1994 The International Bank for Reconstruction
and Development / THE WORLD BANK
1818 H Street, N.W.
Washington, D.C. 20433

The Development in Practice series publishes reviews of the World
Bank's activities in different regions and sectors. It lays particular emphasis
on the progress that is being made and on the policies and practices that
hold the most promise of success in the effort to reduce poverty in the
developing world.

This book is a product of the staff of the World Bank, and the judgments
made herein do not necessarily reflect the view of its Board of Executive
Directors or the countries they represent.

The photograph on the cover was taken in Côte d'Ivoire by Borje Tobiasson
and is used by permission of Panos Pictures.

Library of Congress Cataloging-in-Publication Data
Population and development : implications for the World Bank.
     p.   cm. — (Development in practice)
   Includes bibliographical references.
   ISBN 0-8213-2999-5
   1. Population—Economic aspects.   2. Economic development.
   3. Population—Economic aspects—Developing countries.
   4. International Bank for Reconstruction and Development.
   I. International Bank for Reconstruction and Development.
   II. Series: Development in practice (Washington, D.C.)
   HB849.41.P638   1994
   304.6—dc20   94-31613
                                                              CIP

Contents

Foreword

THE 1994 International Conference on Population and Development is an occasion to reflect on the challenging population issues of this decade and beyond. For the World Bank, this report is the first major review on population since *World Development Report 1984*, which was prepared for the last world population conference.

The report recommends population policies that integrate investments in reproductive health and family planning information with other human resource investments, including those that will reduce the continued high levels of maternal and child mortality in developing countries, increase women's education, and raise their economic and social status. Such investments are beneficial in their own right and will also help to slow rapid population growth.

While financial and technical support needs depend on country-specific conditions, much could be accomplished if governments and aid donors would allocate the resources needed to achieve these goals and if they would place greater emphasis on successful implementation of their projects and on undertaking effective social sector reforms.

The pursuit of sustainable economic growth is also a very important prerequisite for human development and for completion of the demographic transition. Raising of living standards for the large numbers of people being added to the populations of developing countries will not be possible without economic growth. Economic integration, openness in trade, and technology transfer as well as environmental preservation are essential for bringing about sustainable economic development.

Armeane M. Choksi
Vice President
Human Resource Development
and Operations Policy
The World Bank

Acknowledgments

THIS report is the outcome of an extensive review of major population trends and issues in the developing countries and their implications for the World Bank's work in population and related social sectors. The review was requested by the the Bank's Executive Directors to guide the Bank's participation in the 1994 International Conference on Population and Development.

The report was prepared under the general direction of Tom Merrick, senior population adviser, Population, Health, and Nutrition (PHN) Department, in collaboration with other members of that department, including Janet Nassim, Chantal Worzala, Susan Cochrane, Randy Bulatao, Eduard Bos, My Vu, Sharon Russell, and William McGreevey, all of whom contributed to various sections of the report. Martha Ainsworth and Emmanuel Jimenez of the Policy Research Department also contributed to several sections. Dorothy Wexler gave editorial assistance on early drafts of the document.

Comments and guidance on earlier drafts of the report were provided by a World Bank Review Group that included Martha Ainsworth, Bruce Fitzgerald, Althea Hill, Ishrat Z. Husain, Maria Mac Donald, Erik Palstra, Ok Pannenborg, Maryse Pierre-Louise, David Radel, Ronald Ridker, Sandra Rosenhouse, Margaret Saunders, Paul Shaw, Susan Stout, S. K. Sudhakar, and Julianna Weissman. Valuable comments were also provided by other members of the Bank staff, including Alan Berg, Jeffrey Hammer, Peter Heywood, Jane Kirby, Valerie Kozel, Judy Maguire, Peter Moock, Lant Pritchett, George Psacharopoulos, Lyn Squire, James Socknat, Andrew Steer, Jee Peng Tan, and Caby Verzosa.

An outside panel of experts also reviewed draft versions of the report. This group consisted of Mayra Buvinic, Margaret Catley-Carlson, Ronald Freedman, Manuel Urbina Fuentes, Malcolm Potts, Fred Sai, and Jay Satia.

Other comments from outside the Bank were provided by Paula DiPerna, Allen Kelley, Barbara Pillsbury, and John May.

Preparation of the document was managed very ably by Katya Gutierrez of the PHN Department, with assistance from Odell Shoffner. Otilia Nadora, Mely Menciano, and Joan Santini of PHN also assisted in various aspects of the review process. Janet de Merode, director of the Population, Health, and Nutrition Department at the time of writing, provided generous support and guidance.

Executive Summary

ONCE each decade, the global population community pauses, takes stock of itself, and debates the challenging and sometimes controversial issues that lie ahead. At the 1974 World Population Conference in Bucharest, much of the debate centered on how best to slow the high rates of population growth that prevailed in most developing countries. In 1984, the developing countries themselves seized the policy initiative as donor leadership faltered over the abortion controversy. The 1994 International Conference on Population and Development in Cairo is addressing population issues that will take us into the twenty-first century: completing the demographic transition in the world's poorest countries and addressing other demographic issues in countries that have completed that transition; linking population more effectively to core development agendas, particularly those that empower women; and broadening the scope of family planning to address a wider range of reproductive health goals.

There is an emerging consensus, as reflected in the plan of action for the 1994 conference, that population policy objectives should be integrated with broader social development goals and that population program strategies should build on the linkages between demographic behavior and social and economic progress. This consensus is based on the view that interventions which are responsive to individual needs and aspirations are not only better from a humanitarian and social development perspective but also more effective in lowering fertility than are programs driven by top-down demographic targets.

This report examines the changes in population dynamics and in the policy environment that have produced this consensus and explores their policy and operational implications for the World Bank's population work. The report has five core messages:

- Slowing of population growth is still a high priority in the poorest countries.[1] High birth rates and very young populations make it more difficult to reduce poverty, invest in human resources, and pursue sustainable economic development. For individuals, unplanned and poorly timed pregnancies pose grave health risks. Where private markets fail to provide information and services for fertility regulation, governments have an important role to play in addressing the population objectives of slowing growth rates and reducing unwanted fertility.

- Population policy should be integrated with social policies that address a range of poverty reduction and human development objectives. Particular emphasis should be placed on better infant and child health, education of girls, and overall improvements in the status of women. These measures bring important benefits in their own right, and experience shows that they are more effective in reducing high birth rates than policies that focus narrowly on fertility reduction alone.

- Population programs should focus on providing the poor with access to high-quality, user-oriented services that offer a range of choices in addressing fertility regulation and other reproductive health needs. This approach is more likely to change reproductive behavior and to improve individual health and welfare, particularly when accompanied by effective information about the benefits of such services.

- Country-specific strategies are required. Public sector interventions will need to take into account individual country needs, cultural values, and financial and institutional constraints. In many instances, the appropriate role of government will be to ensure that adequate information is available and to remove obstacles to the effective functioning of the private sector. In some cases, particularly in poor countries that do not yet have service-delivery infrastructure and institutional capacity, selective investments may be required to remedy these gaps, particularly where the public sector is more generally involved in health finance and service delivery and where reproductive health and family planning services are limited.

■ In addition to population growth, other demographic issues
have taken on increased social, economic, and political
significance: urbanization, international migration, and aging.
These demographic issues cut across a wide range of sectors—
health, education, infrastructure, social security, trade—that are
beyond the scope of this report. Understanding and determining
how the Bank should respond to them in coming decades
should be addressed through research, sector work, and policy
dialogue.[2]

These messages are based on a review of demographic trends and of their
policy and operational implications for the World Bank and borrower countries, including the issue of unwanted pregnancies and their consequences,
and the role of the public sector in population. It also provides a framework
for articulating country-specific, integrated approaches to population policies
and programs. The main conclusions are that major demographic challenges
remain, that public sector interventions are warranted, that integrated approaches are needed, and that the World Bank has a role to play in these
efforts.

Major Demographic Challenges Remain

Population in developing countries will grow more during this decade (by
more than 80 million people each year) than ever before. This surge in population growth, which began when death rates declined earlier and faster than
birth rates, has begun to abate as more and more countries experience the transition to lower fertility. This has lowered population growth *rates*. However,
countries will continue to experience very large absolute increases in numbers
during the next two to three decades. These large absolute increases further
exacerbate the difficulties faced by poor countries in providing social services, creating jobs, and achieving sustainable economic growth.

Fertility rates in developing countries have declined by as much as half,
but the number of couples in reproductive ages has more than doubled. As
fertility declines toward the replacement level (the level at which couples
have the number of children required to replace themselves, that is, about
two), population growth does not immediately decline to zero. Large absolute
increases in population can persist for several decades. This phenomenon, referred to by demographers as *population momentum,* is a facet of the youthful
age structures of developing-country populations, which in turn reflect high
birth rates in past decades. Population momentum is a major challenge, not
just for poor countries with high birth rates but also for the world at large.

Population momentum can be reduced by investments to increase educa-

tional opportunities, to expand reproductive health and family planning information and services, and to reduce maternal and child mortality. The *timing* of
these investments is critical to offsetting momentum. Slowing population
growth sooner rather than later could reduce future global population size by 2
billion–3 billion when global population finally stabilizes at the end of the
next century.[3] Delaying such investments will only add to the ultimate costs
of poverty reduction.

Public Sector Interventions Are Warranted

Public sector actions to slow high rates of population growth are warranted in
poor countries where population growth hampers efforts to invest in human
resources, reduce poverty, and protect the environment. In countries that are
still at early stages of or have yet to begin transitions to lower fertility, rapid
population growth is eroding the quality of investments in human resources
whether it be at the community or the family level. These effects vary in their
nature and severity among and within countries, and the evidence about externalities resulting from rapid population growth does not support across-the-
board generalizations about the adverse effects of population growth that once
characterized the population debate.

Country-specific evidence suggests that rapid population growth is inhibiting investments in the social sectors; for example, many countries still experiencing rapid increases in the size of the school-age population have been
caught on a treadmill trying to keep up with ever-increasing numbers, while
countries that have experienced fertility decline have been able to improve the
quality of education and increase access to underserved groups. Similar corro-
sive effects appear in other social sectors, in job creation, and in the management of natural resources. At the household and individual levels, large families invest less in their children, with a clear bias against girls that perpetuates
the cycle of high fertility and low income; smaller families invest more in
their children, and girls are more likely to observe their mothers in higher-
status roles.

The rationales for public sector involvement in family planning and reproductive health are not limited to poor countries with high fertility. In fact,
there are broader grounds for public action with respect to overcoming market
failures that deprive individuals (particularly the poor) of reproductive health/
family planning information and services. The timing, spacing, and degree to
which pregnancies are wanted, independent of their total number, have important impacts on maternal and child health. This health impact on women and
their families, combined with failures in the market for health and fertility
regulation, provides an impetus for public action even where demographic

concerns are absent and can be an equally compelling reason for those actions when demographic concerns are present.

The appropriate role for government depends on local circumstances and needs. Where government plays a more active role in the provision of health services, reproductive health should be included among them. Where the private sector is expected to play a more prominent role, government involvement may still be required to provide financial support or to remove legal and regulatory obstacles to information and services, including medical regulations that unnecessarily increase the amount of time and money that individuals have to expend. Even if, as *World Development Report 1993* suggested, government has a social interest in making family planning available, its responsibility lies in ensuring access to information and services rather than in acting in every instance as financier and provider. Where the case is strong for public subsidy of low-income and rural groups, and more broadly for subsidy of family planning information, the government role may not necessarily be in providing services but in encouraging the most efficient private/public sector mix.

Integrated Approaches Are Needed in Population Policy

On balance, an earlier completion of the demographic transition will make it easier for poor countries to tackle the difficult challenges they face in reducing poverty among their populations and in protecting the natural resources on which they depend. Although slower population growth will not solve other development problems, poverty reduction through a broad range of human resource investments, including family planning, is the most likely way to speed up the demographic transition and achieve these other objectives.

Accelerated declines in fertility in East and Southeast Asia (Korea, Indonesia, Taiwan [China], Thailand) and in Latin American (Brazil, Colombia, Mexico) were accompanied by important social and economic changes. Fertility declines have been most rapid in countries where key social policies complemented population policies. Improvements in the status of women through increased education, access to credit and earnings opportunities, and breaking down of legal and cultural barriers to women's participation in the development process are important examples. Motivation to have smaller families and to regulate fertility was also increased by broader social development efforts, economic growth, and improved living standards. Experience has also shown that high-quality, user-oriented services that provide people with a range of choices in addressing their reproductive health needs are most likely to change reproductive behavior and to improve individual health and welfare, particularly when accompanied by effective information about the benefits of those services.

Debate has continued about the relative importance of factors of supply (family planning information and services) and demand (the effect of increased education on motivation to have smaller families) in fertility decline. The answer is not "either/or" but rather "both" and, even better, a balance of both that is responsive to the specific needs and conditions of different countries at different levels of the demographic transition and socioeconomic development. Over time, the interplay between demand and supply changes, as countries move from high to low fertility. This requires continuing effort to reassess the mix of policies and programs at the country level.

Quality of care is an increasingly important program issue. Poor quality, as reflected in an inadequate mix of methods, poor counseling, and lack of courteous attention to clients, can have a particularly erosive effect, especially as countries move into the middle stages of their fertility transitions. In contrast, high-quality services often stimulate further demand as satisfied clients communicate their experiences by word of mouth. Method mix has implications for client satisfaction as well as for the demographic effectiveness of programs. Programs that rely too heavily on sterilization, for example, do not serve the needs of younger couples who want to delay or space births. In many instances, public sector clinics offering only sterilization are underused, while private clinics that offer a full range of reproductive health services are generally very busy, even when they charge for services.

As demographic conditions change, borrower-country needs are becoming more and more diverse. Reproductive health and family planning programs have taken hold, have adapted over time, and are meeting changing and expanding needs related to fertility regulation, control and prevention of reproductive tract infections, and safe motherhood. Borrower countries themselves are identifying a wider span of needs. Many are concerned about other population issues such as aging, rapid urbanization, and international migration. Responses to both the causes and consequences of population problems have to be tailored to the specific conditions of borrower countries.

The provision of reproductive health and family planning services requires modest investments in comparison with countries' other health and development needs. Public financing and service provision should be targeted on underserved groups, the poor in particular. In some countries, the need for expanded information and services could be met by reallocating public expenditures away from activities that could be addressed better by the private sector.

The governments of the poorest developing countries may not have sufficient resources to finance and provide the services to meet these needs. Donors can play a role, but there are also limits to what they may be able to provide. In all cases, attention needs to be given to efficiency gains in the provision of services, including those that derive from involvement of private providers, and to mechanisms to recover costs or provide services through commercial channels in situations where users are able to pay for them.

The World Bank Has an Important Role to Play

These challenges have been putting greater and more diverse demands on the Bank. An increasing number of countries actively seek to work with the Bank on population issues—and borrow from it as well. Bank managers and staff have improved their capacity to work with borrowers, other donors, and nongovernmental organizations in formulating creative population projects to meet the diverse needs that typify this sector, but this capacity to respond to borrower demand should be strengthened further and is an important issue for continued expansion of Bank population work. At the policy level, there is strong commitment to an integrated approach to population, as illustrated in the communiqué issued at the April 1994 meeting of the Joint Ministerial Committee of the Boards of Governors of the World Bank and the International Monetary Fund (see box 1).

BOX 1. DEVELOPMENT COMMITTEE COMMUNIQUÉ

Ministers believe that integrated population policy in developing countries must recognize the links between economic growth, population, poverty reduction, health, investment in human resources, and environmental degradation. All couples and individuals have the right to decide freely and *responsibly* the number and spacing of their children. Family planning is only one of the available instruments and needs to be seen in the broader context of changing social patterns and the increased awareness of women's role. Population programs are therefore becoming increasingly diverse, depending on the stage of the demographic transition in each country. Moreover, experience demonstrates that improved education and employment prospects (particularly for girls), improved health, and increased income all tend to reduce the birth rate. Institutional arrangements for the delivery of services may need to be strengthened and must be tailored to local conditions and needs, taking full advantage of available nongovernmental and private sector organizations. They must pay full regard to the social and cultural traditions of each country.

The Bank has supported a broad range of policy and program measures to bring about the health and welfare benefits of fertility regulation and speed up the transition to lower fertility. These measures include efforts to increase the survival chances of mothers and children, to expand female education, and to improve women's status, in addition to provision of family planning services. Bank support of public and private sector efforts to achieve these objectives are generally targeted on the poor, who may lack information or access to services because of market failure or inability to pay.

Total new commitments for population, health, and nutrition amounted to $1.8 billion in fiscal 1993. The Bank has increased its investments in maternal health and safe motherhood tenfold since the inception of the Safe Motherhood Initiative in 1986, through family planning and other efforts to deal with the unsafe abortions and obstetric emergencies that claim the lives of 500,000 women each year in developing countries. There were also investments of $1.9 billion in education, which the Bank increasingly targets on keeping girls in school. Overall, the share of the Bank's lending portfolio devoted to the social sectors has grown from 6 to 16 percent in the last five years.

Over the last five years the Bank has become one of the leading international financiers of reproductive health and family planning information and services. The annual dollar total of family planning components in new loans has more than doubled since the mid-1980s to around $200 million in recent years. The mix of projects has changed from a few large projects devoted mainly to construction of facilities to a larger number of more targeted projects addressing a range of programmatic needs, including contraceptive procurement, training, social marketing, and management information systems, as well as equipment and facilities, all key elements of successful family planning and reproductive health programs. There are currently more than seventy population and family planning–related projects in the Bank's active portfolio; they represent more than $1 billion in total loans and credits for population work. Fifty countries in all stages of the fertility transition, from Nigeria to Indonesia, are represented in this portfolio.

The Cairo Conference offers a special opportunity to readdress the population issue and, by so doing, to make substantial gains in reducing poverty and improving welfare. Rather than attempting to cover everything, the Bank will emphasize the following:

- Working with borrower countries and other donors to mobilize public and private sector financing and other resources required to meet the growing demand for reproductive health and family planning services and to expand educational opportunities
- Assisting borrower countries through their own strategic

investments, emphasizing appropriate infrastructure,
institutional capacity, and effective management of social sector
activities
■ Coordinating the mobilization of resources as much as possible
  with the effort to supply the core package of essential health
  services called for in *World Development Report 1993* and
  applying that report's guidance on health finance and
  management in working with borrowers on reproductive health
  projects
■ Strengthening its skill mix in needed technical areas, applying
  its available capacity for financial and economic analysis in the
  sector, and working collaboratively with other donors and
  specialized agencies that have complementary skills and
  capacities
■ Using its analytical capacity and supporting research to broaden
  the scope of population policy through better understanding of
  the linkages among population change, reproductive health, and
  the Bank's broader human development and poverty alleviation
  agendas and recognizing more effectively in country strategies
  and other analytical documents the interconnections between
  population dynamics and successful achievement of those
  agendas.

Ultimately, borrower countries themselves—their governments and
people—have the major responsibility to address population challenges. Very
little will be done unless high priority is accorded to both population and social development agendas and until governments demonstrate the political
will to move ahead with them. The Bank, through policy dialogue, can help to
focus attention on these challenges and, through strengthened relationships
with donors, nongovernmental organizations, and grassroots organizations,
can help governments define and pursue strategies for meeting them. It stands
ready to do so.

Notes

1. The main focus of this report is on countries that are still in the process
of completing their demographic transitions. However, the report also touches
on reproductive health/family planning issues in new borrower countries in
Eastern Europe and the former U.S.S.R.
2. The Bank is conducting a parallel review of international migration issues and their implications for Bank operations. Also, a review of aging and

social security issues is being conducted by the Development Economics Vice Presidential Unit (see World Bank 1994). The Bank also addresses a wide range of health, education, and urban issues in its research, sector work, and policy dialogue.

3. A billion is 1,000 million.

CHAPTER ONE

Introduction

$\mathbf{T}$HE ultimate objective of population policy is to improve human welfare at both the individual and societal levels, for the present as well as future generations. For that reason, concern about the effects of rapid population growth and high fertility on societies and individuals has been the central focus of population policy over the past two decades. For most of that time, population policy has meant policy to reduce population growth by promoting family planning. A significant number of borrower countries have this as an explicit population policy objective, and many have specific fertility-reduction targets. Although slowing of population growth rates in poor countries remains an important development objective, broader approaches to policy are now seen as both more consistent with underlying individual and societal welfare goals and more effective in guiding the actions needed to achieve them.

Broadening the Scope of Population Policy

Over the last twenty-five years, efforts to slow rapid population growth have occupied the largest part of the population agenda of the Bank and its borrowers. Socioeconomic improvements and rising use of contraceptives have accelerated the pace of transitions to low fertility in many developing countries (see figure 1-1). Nonetheless, these transitions are still far from complete, and they have hardly started in many poor countries. Moreover, high birth rates in the past have built up substantial population growth momentum, which creates very large increases in absolute numbers of people despite lower growth rates.

Figure 1-1.   Fertility Rates since 1960

Total fertility rate (births per woman)

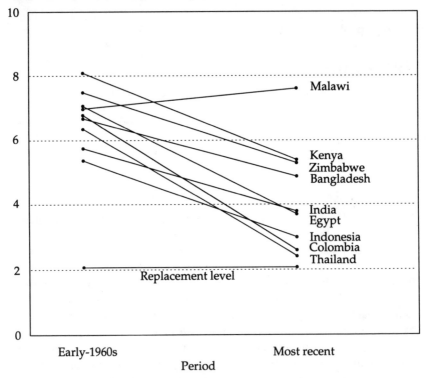

Source: 1960s, United Nations 1993; most recent, Bos and others 1994.

Although the narrower view of population policy in terms of supplying family planning and reducing fertility has served to focus attention and resources, this issue has been the subject of considerable rethinking during the 1980s (see Sen, Germain, and Chen 1994). One reason is that the narrower view has tended to separate or isolate population from the broader spectrum of development concerns, ignoring the important role that social and economic changes play in creating demand for smaller families and for family planning. Second, the cultural and political sensitivity of the population issue, particularly when it is perceived as population control, has inhibited rather than encouraged government and donor involvement in the sector. More recently, women's groups and reproductive health advocates have criticized policies aimed at promoting family planning in order to control population growth on grounds that the delivery of services is likely to be driven more by the desire to attain population growth targets than by concerns about individual reproductive health needs and that such policies may infringe on individual reproductive rights (see box 1-1; Dixon-Mueller 1993).

This report articulates integrated approaches to population policy. Without denying the importance of family planning for achieving fertility decline, these integrated approaches recognize the significant roles that better health and improved socioeconomic conditions play in shaping reproductive decisions. They are also more consistent with the view that the objective of population policy is to increase individual and family welfare as well as to pursue such societal goals as lowering population growth rates. Integration is addressed at two levels. The first involves integration of population objectives within a broad range of social policy goals relating to family welfare, investment in human resources (particularly education of girls), and other measures to improve the role and status of women.

The second level of integration involves delivery of family planning as part of the essential package of reproductive health services described in *World Development Report 1993: Investing in Health* and in the forthcoming Bank best-practice paper on women's health and nutrition (Tinker and others 1994; World Bank 1993e). The essential package includes prevention and management of unwanted pregnancies, safe pregnancy and delivery services, prevention and management of reproductive tract infections and sexually transmitted diseases (including HIV/AIDS), promotion of positive health practices (safe sex, male involvement in family planning, adequate nutrition, and so forth), and prevention of practices that are harmful to reproductive health (for example, providing less health care for girls than for boys).

A Country-Specific Framework for Assessing Policy and Program Needs

An added challenge is to determine the appropriate policies and programs for increasingly diverse country settings. Because of the great diversity among borrower countries, no single prescription of the "right" policy and programmatic mix is possible. Rather, strategies need to address the complexity and diversity of conditions both within and between countries. These conditions have many roots.

First, the institutional and organizational capacity of countries varies substantially. Some countries (Indonesia, for example) now have well-developed institutional mechanisms for delivery of reproductive health and family planning services as well as for implementation of other social policies; others,

---

BOX 1-1. TARGETS, INCENTIVES, AND REPRODUCTIVE RIGHTS

Targets and Incentives. In many countries whose governments seek to slow population growth, targets have been used to guide programs, and financial incentives and/or sanctions have been employed to stimulate sluggish bureaucracies to action or to change individual behavior patterns. The pros and cons of targets and incentives have been debated for two decades (see Cleland and Mauldin 1991; Ross and Isaacs 1988). Both are a common feature of Asian family planning programs (for example, in Bangladesh, India, and Viet Nam). Incentive payments to individuals have proved to be effective in stimulating clients to use specific methods, particularly at the initial stages of program development. Community-level incentives contributed to considerable increase in family planning use in Thailand and Indonesia.

The record on incentives for providers is more problematic, particularly when they have been tied to demographic targets. In addition to the high cost of these incentives and problems of administration and potential mismanagement, concerns arise about ethical issues and infringement on individual reproductive rights. Providers seeking incentives linked to targets for a particular method may pay inadequate attention to client needs. Proponents of incentives for clients, on the one hand, argue that such payments are needed to offset the social costs of high fertility. Critics, on the other hand, are concerned that even when the amounts of cash payments (or their equivalent in goods) to clients are small, the risk that individuals are, in fact, being coerced is real. They doubt that societal costs warrant coercion or actions that would harm the health of individuals (Sanderson and Tan 1993).

Another argument against incentives is that resources could be used more fruitfully in other ways, such as to improve the quality and access to services or to invest in informational efforts to inform clients about how services can meet their reproductive health needs. The benefits derived from improved services are corroborated by a growing body of research

---

including many countries in Sub-Saharan Africa, still have only limited institutional capacity for these efforts. Second, financial capacity varies greatly, with some countries facing financial constraints so severe that it would be difficult for them to provide services without external funding, whereas others have progressed to where they should be able to implement strategies for recovery of costs and mobilization of local resources to sustain programs over the long run.

A third aspect of this diversity is demographic. Three decades ago most developing countries were just beginning the transition to lower fertility and

that verifies that people are more likely to use, and even pay for, services that are of high quality and responsive to their needs (see Jain 1989; Phillips and others 1993).

This view is further supported by the point that the demographic targets set by most countries would in fact be exceeded if high-quality services were extended to those who say they want to limit or space births but are not using a method of fertility regulation (Sinding 1993). Many consumers say they are not using a method for reasons such as fear of side effects, cultural or religious objections to certain methods, or concerns about the reactions of spouses and other relatives, all of which reflect limitations in the choice of options or poor counseling. Because much of this unmet need reflects poor services, concentrating on service quality may be the most effective way there is of reaching demographic targets.

Safeguarding reproductive rights. The debate about demographic objectives extends to how government should employ demographic information to shape policy or guide and evaluate programs. Some reproductive health advocates oppose any form of demographic orientation in family planning and argue that family planning should be approached only in the context of reproductive health services. This appears to be in conflict with the view that slower population growth is a valid developmental objective in poor countries. In fact, it is not. The risks associated with demographically oriented policies should be recognized. These risks can be reduced by shifting the programmatic orientation of population programs to provision of safe and effective services that meet individual reproductive health needs. Targets, if needed for effective program management, need to be stated in terms of the proportion of individuals who are provided with quality services rather than the relative or absolute reductions in total fertility or population growth rates. Independent monitoring mechanisms should be set up to ensure that reproductive health and reproductive rights are protected.

mortality. Some countries are now well along in those transitions, while others are still at very early stages. For example, in Rwanda and Malawi total fertility is above six children, infant and maternal mortality rates are still high even by developing-country standards, contraceptive use is negligible, and access to family planning and reproductive health services is very limited. Further along on this spectrum are countries such as Brazil and China, which have experienced rapid demographic transitions but must still deal with significant reproductive health problems, including high levels of contraceptive failure and high levels of unsafe abortion.

For countries just starting their transitions, timing is also a critical consideration in articulating sector strategies. For those countries to get ahead of the wave of population momentum, significant investments to expand reproductive health and family planning services, educational opportunities, and other key social services have to be made *now*. Population momentum also affects countries in the middle stages of the demographic transition. The challenge is to design and implement approaches that take account of the needs of particular countries and the time required for different interventions to take effect. Sound macroeconomic policies are also needed, because without economic growth countries will not be able to support the larger numbers resulting from demographic momentum. Without strategic approaches that recognize the interconnections between demographic, social, and economic changes, development may stall. Countries could end up on a demographic treadmill, running faster to keep up with population growth and incurring added costs over the long run because of large increases in the numbers generated by momentum.

Further diversity in country needs derives from the entry of new Bank borrower countries in Eastern Europe and Central Asia. Some of these countries have completed the demographic transition, but many of them still need to make the public aware of reproductive health options and to develop basic service infrastructure. Others need to expand access to contraceptive supplies and improve counseling programs in order to improve quality and expand choice in fertility regulation—for example, in Ukraine, fertility is actually below replacement level, but there is substantial dependence on abortion.

Table 1-1 provides a framework for assessing the variety of country needs at both levels of integration described above: reproductive health/family planning programs and broader social policy. The framework is simpler than some of the other frameworks that have been developed to classify countries according to where they stand in their fertility transition (see USAID 1989; World Bank 1993b). However, this framework adds a social-development dimension that is absent from other frameworks and thus better emphasizes the integrated approaches to reproductive health/family planning and broader social policy recommended here.

The table presents indicators to measure countries' progress in the demographic transition and in social development. The table is divided vertically into three segments according to the levels of those indicators. Thus, countries with total fertility rates above 6 are considered to be emergent in their fertility transitions, those with rates between 3 and 6 are classified as transitional, while those with rates below 3 are grouped in the advanced category. Similarly, countries with adult female literacy rates below 40 percent are considered emergent in terms of social setting, those with rates between 40 and 80 percent are classified as transitional, and those with rates over 80 percent are advanced. To simplify the presentation, the setting breakdowns are limited to this pair of demographic and social indicators. Other indicators of reproductive health and women's status are listed in the table for illustration, and an even broader list would be required for a full assessment of country needs.

The table also lists selected policy options corresponding to each stage. Thus countries in emergent demographic settings generally would need to make investments in basic reproductive health and family planning infrastructure and to build institutional capacity, while those at advanced stages would focus more on reaching underserved groups and encouraging sustainable financing strategies. Countries in emergent social settings would emphasize investments in universal primary education, while those that are advanced would aim at such actions as social safety nets for underserved groups and improvements in quality. The table also allows for situations in which a country is more advanced in demographic terms than in social development, or vice versa. Where such imbalances exist, countries need to put greater emphasize on policy options listed for the earlier stages of the neglected sector. The approach also applies to imbalances within countries: for example, strategies that address differential conditions in northern and southern India, northeastern and southern Brazil, or northern and southern Nigeria.

Table 1-2 provides some country examples to illustrate this. Generally, one would expect that countries at a given stage of the demographic transition should be at similar levels of social development (corresponding to cells along the diagonal of the table). Thus most of Sub-Saharan Africa is listed as being emergent for both demographic and social settings. However, Kenya is listed as having moved from emergent in the 1970s to transitional today. Indonesia was transitional during the 1970s but has moved to advanced on both scales today.

The matrix highlights some examples of the imbalances mentioned above. Bangladesh, northern India, and a number of other countries that have advanced more rapidly in fertility decline than in social development are listed as transitional in fertility but emergent in social setting. They need to put greater emphasis on policy actions corresponding to the emergent level of social settings. In contrast, the Philippines is advanced in terms of social setting but needs to emphasize policy options appropriate to the transitional level of the demographic setting. The case of Mexico during the 1960s provides a parallel example of such an imbalance; when Mexico changed its policy on family planning during the late-1970s, it moved quickly from the emergent to the advanced stage of the demographic transition. The fact that countries have completed their transitions to low fertility does not guarantee that they have made equal progress in other aspects of reproductive health. For example, Brazil is listed in the advanced demographic setting category but has ad-

Table 1-1. Demographic and Social Indicators and Policy Framework for Emergent, Transitional, and Advanced Settings
(percent)

Indicator and policy framework	Emergent	Transitional	Advanced
Indicator			
Demographic setting			
Total fertility rate[a]	>6	6–3	<3
Contraceptive prevalence[b]	<15	15–60	60–80
Under-five mortality rate[c]	>200	200–20	<20
Maternal mortality rate[d]	>500	500–30	<30
Antenatal care[e]	<30	30–90	>90
Social setting			
Adult female literacy[f]	<40	40–80	>80
Educational attainment[g]			
Completed primary	<30	30–90	>90
Completed secondary	<10	10–50	>50
Women's access to credit[h]	Rare	Expanding	Widespread

Policy framework

Demographic setting	Invest in (1) infrastructure and institutional capacity for basic package; (2) pilot approaches to service delivery; and (3) information and public education.	Extend basic package to underserved groups; involve private sector; and address quality issues, legal and regulatory obstacles, and cost recovery.	Target subsidies to underserved groups; implement sustainable financing; maintain quality; and close remaining reproductive health gaps.
Social setting	Invest in (1) universal primary education; and (2) adult literacy and other initiatives for school leavers; and initiate credit schemes and other initiatives.	Expand access to secondary education; expand programs for school leavers; and expand credit and other programs for women.	Target underserved groups; and remove remaining obstacles to women's full economic and social participation.

a. Births per woman aged fifteen to forty-nine.
b. Percentage of reproductive-age women in unions practicing fertility regulation.
c. Deaths up to age five per 1,000 live births.
d. Maternal deaths per 100,000 live births.
e. Percentage of pregnant women receiving tetanus immunizations, micronutrients, and screening at least once during pregnancy.
f. Percentage of women over age twenty who are literate.
g. Percentage of women aged twenty to twenty-four who have completed primary level or secondary education and higher.
h. A qualitative statement.

Table 1-2.   Matrix of Countries in Various Stages of Policy Transition, by Demographic and Social Setting

Social setting	Demographic setting		
	Emergent	Transitional	Advanced
Emergent	Kenya during 1970s, most of Sub-Saharan Africa, Pakistan	Bangladesh, Egypt, Morocco, North India	—
Transitional	Mexico during 1960s	Indonesia during 1970s, Kenya, Turkey	Brazil
Advanced	—	Philippines	Colombia, Indonesia, Mexico, South India, Thailand

— None.

Note: 1990s unless otherwise noted.

vanced less than Mexico and Colombia on reproductive health and social indicators. Under such conditions, a third dimension might be added to address imbalances in reproductive health conditions in demographically advanced countries that have made more progress on women's social status than in reproductive health (Ukraine and Russian Federation, for example).

Although the policy framework in tables 1-1 and 1-2 is highly simplified, it does highlight four important points that need to be recognized in assessing evidence and drawing policy conclusions about fertility decline: (1) country needs are diverse and vary according to social and demographic settings, (2) needs change over the course of demographic and social transitions, (3) the relative weights assigned to policy options both in reproductive health/family planning and in broader social policy arenas should reflect the diversity and changing nature of country needs, and (4) most important, no single set of policy prescriptions will be adequate across the complex and diverse range of conditions that prevail among Bank borrower countries. Further discussion of the specific policy options suggested by these country examples can be found in chapter 6, where a series of boxes describe country cases at each of the three levels of demographic transition.

Goals and Structure of the Report

The report has three goals. First, through the exploration of the Bank's approach and comparative advantage, it will help the Bank to rethink its strategies and also inform other agencies and donors in the population field about the Bank's potential. Second, the report's proposed agenda for action should help set the direction for the Bank's investments in population work over the next five to ten years. Finally, these recommendations should provide a basis for dialogue on policy and program issues with member countries, particularly those in which population is or could be an important domain of Bank operations.

The report is organized around three sets of questions:

- How demographic conditions have changed over the past two decades, specifically in terms of major trends (chapter 2) and whether their implications for economic development, poverty reduction, individual health and welfare, and the environment warrant government intervention in population (chapter 3).
- What has been learned about the relative importance of supply and demand factors in fertility transitions (chapter 4) and how to apply those lessons through more integrated approaches to population policies and programs: first, by integrating population into broader social and economic policies that are beneficial in their own right and contribute to slowing of population growth rates (chapter 5), and second, by integrating family planning into an essential package of reproductive health services (chapter 6). At both levels, the question of public and private sector actions to accomplish these goals is addressed.
- How the Bank is responding to these changing needs: what it does well, what it is not doing that should be done, how it could improve its operational capacity, and how it could work more effectively with others in this field (chapter 7).

Detailed information on other donors in the population field, on Bank lending for population and how it is counted, and on earlier reviews of Bank population work are presented in appendixes.

CHAPTER TWO

Developing-Country Demographic Trends

●

$\mathbf{P}$OPULATION growth rates have begun to slow in many developing countries. The surge in population growth that began when death rates declined earlier and faster than birth rates has begun to stabilize as more and more developing countries experience the transition to lower fertility. Even with slower growth *rates*, however, developing countries continue to experience large absolute increases in population. In fact, their populations are expected to increase by more people during the 1990s than during any previous decade. The reason for this surge in population is the combination of still high fertility rates and the youthful age structures in those countries, which result in many more births than deaths. This combination holds the potential for adding several billion more people to the populations of developing countries. How large those populations eventually will be depends mainly on the speed of their transition to low fertility.

Although the global picture is one of continued growth, substantial variation is evident among regions. Rapid demographic changes are taking place in many areas, while shifts are more gradual in other, mainly poorer, regions. Table 2-1 shows that the largest absolute increases in population from 1950 to 1990 took place in Asia, where almost six out of every ten of the world's people live. At the same time, the largest percentage increases in population occurred in Africa—which has nearly tripled in population since 1950—and in Latin America. The populations of Europe and countries of the former U.S.S.R. are declining rapidly as a percentage of the world's population, from 23 to 15 percent.

Table 2-1. Population and Percentage Distribution, by Geographic Region, 1950–90

Region	Population (millions)			Percentage of world population		
	1950	1970	1990	1950	1970	1990
World	2,516	3,697	5,267	100.0	100.0	100.0
Less-industrial countries	1,684	2,648	4,052	66.9	71.7	76.9
More-industrial countries	832	1,049	1,215	33.1	28.3	23.1
Africa	222	363	628	8.9	9.8	11.9
East Africa	98	162	274	3.9	4.4	5.2
West Africa	72	118	214	2.9	3.2	4.1
North Africa	52	83	140	2.1	2.2	2.6
America	331	510	715	13.2	13.8	13.6
Latin America and the Caribbean	165	284	435	6.6	7.7	8.3
North America	166	226	280	6.6	6.1	5.3
Asia	1,376	2,102	3,107	54.7	56.9	59.0
East and Southeast Asia	853	1,274	1,788	33.9	34.5	34.0
South Asia	481	754	1,186	19.1	20.4	22.5
Southwest Asia	42	74	133	1.7	2.0	2.5
Europe and U.S.S.R.	572	703	790	22.7	19.0	15.0
Oceania	13	27	27	0.5	0.5	0.5

Source: For 1950 and 1970, United Nations 1993b; for 1990, Bos and others 1994.

Variation in population growth rates differs from the pattern in absolute increases (see figure 2-1). Africa, which has only one-fifth the population of Asia, is currently increasing by around 3 percent a year and is the only region of the world where growth rates are actually higher than they were in 1965–70. Asia's population growth rates have declined to below 2 percent a year. The world as a whole is growing at 1.7 percent a year, at which rate the population will double in forty years.

Status of Demographic Transitions

Underlying this surge in population is a process demographers refer to as the *demographic transition*. Prior to the onset of this process, population grows very slowly because high death rates offset the high birth rates characteristic

Figure 2-1.   Average Annual Growth Rates, 1965–70 and 1990–95

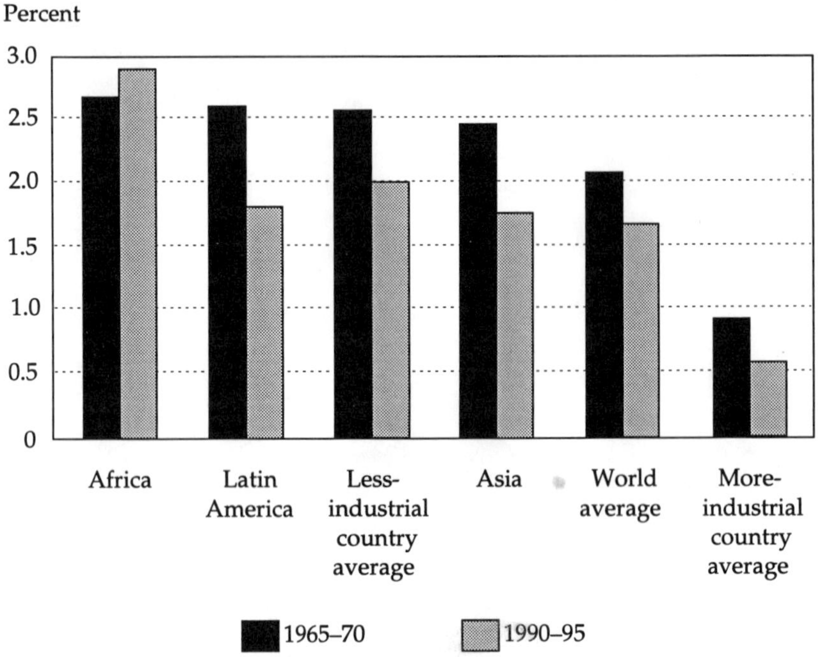

Percent

| | 1965–70 | | 1990–95 |

Source: 1965–70, United Nations 1993; 1990–95, Bos and others 1994.

of preindustrial societies. Periodic fluctuations in population growth did occur in different regions before the demographic transition began, but the global balance was such that population grew very slowly. In Europe, the demographic transition got under way at about the time of the Industrial Revolution, which gradually brought improved living conditions, followed by advances in public health and medical technology, which together resulted in declining mortality. Initially birth rates remained steady or even increased, but eventually the social, economic, and cultural changes occurring at the time also brought declines in fertility. It was this lag between the onset of declines in fertility and mortality that accelerated population growth during the demographic transitions of European countries.

The main differences between demographic transitions in Europe and those now occurring in developing countries have been the levels of fertility and mortality at the start of the decline and the pace of change during the transition. First, fertility in developing countries has been higher than it was in

Europe at the start of the transition. The reason fertility was initially lower in preindustrial Europe was because people married later and a significant proportion of women never married. Second, mortality in developing countries had already declined to lower levels by the start of their demographic transitions than had Europe's and continued to decline very rapidly after 1950, reflecting not only gradual changes in living conditions and improvements in public health but also twentieth-century measures to control infectious diseases and other interventions, which especially reduced infant and child mortality.

These differences are illustrated in figure 2-2, which compares the demographic transitions in Sweden and Mexico. In Sweden, the pattern of less universal and later marriage had already reduced the birth rate when the death rate started to decline, resulting in a rate between 30 and 35 per thousand population. By contrast, Mexico started with a higher birth rate that declined slowly and a death rate that started at the same level but dropped more rapidly, leading to faster population growth. The result of such differences throughout the developing world is that the gap between birth rates and death rates has been greater and population growth has consequently been higher.

Developing countries vary considerably with regard to where they are in the demographic transition. Some have nearly completed the transition (notably, China and several other Asian countries), others are in the midst of it, with fertility at intermediate levels (several Latin American countries), and some have yet to start (much of Sub-Saharan Africa). Table 2-2 summarizes trends in mortality and fertility indicators. Considerable divergence is noticeable among, as well as within, regions, indicating the different stages of the demographic transition that have been reached.

Population Momentum

As fertility declines toward the replacement level (the level at which couples have the number of children required to replace themselves, that is, about two), population growth does not immediately decline to zero. In fact, the number of births will often continue to be high for several decades, and the absolute increase in the number of people will remain high. This phenomenon, referred to by demographers as *population momentum*, is a facet of the youthful age structures typical of populations in developing countries, which in turn reflect fertility and mortality rates of the past decades.[1] Because of population momentum, the full effect of lower fertility on the growth and age structure of a population takes several decades to be felt. Before smaller birth cohorts born recently make their way through the age structure, larger birth

Table 2-2. Total Fertility Rate and Life Expectancy, by Geographic Region, 1950–55 to 1990–95

Region	Total fertility rate[a]			Life expectancy at birth		
	1950–55	1970–75	1990–95	1950–55	1970–75	1990–95
World	5.0	4.5	3.1	46	58	66
Less-industrial countries	6.2	5.4	3.4	41	55	63
More-industrial countries	2.8	2.2	1.8	66	71	75
Africa	6.7	6.6	5.7	38	46	54
South and East Africa	6.7	6.5	6.0	36	45	52
Middle and West Africa	6.6	6.7	6.1	36	43	51
North Africa	6.8	6.4	4.3	42	51	62
America	4.7	3.7	2.7	60	65	72
Latin America and the Caribbean	5.9	5.0	3.1	51	61	68
Northern America	3.5	2.0	2.1	69	72	77
Asia	5.9	5.1	3.0	41	56	65
East and Southeast Asia	5.9	4.7	2.3	42	60	68
South Asia	6.1	5.8	4.0	39	50	60
Southwest Asia	6.8	6.0	4.6	43	57	66
Europe and U.S.S.R.	2.7	2.3	1.8	65	71	73
Oceania	3.8	3.2	2.4	61	67	73

a. Births per woman aged fifteen to forty-nine.
Source: For 1950–55 and 1970–75, United Nations 1993b; for 1990–95, Bos and others 1994.

Figure 2-2.   **Birth and Death Rates in Sweden and Mexico, Various Years**

Rate per 1,000 population

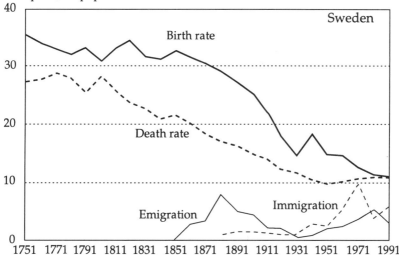

Rate per 1,000 population

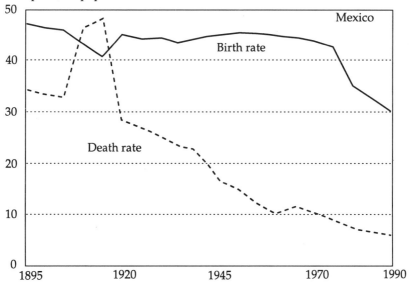

Source: Merrick and others 1989.

cohorts from the past will mean large increases in the number of women of reproductive age and in the number of young adults entering working ages. The combination of above-replacement fertility and population momentum poses an immediate challenge for housing and other types of social infrastructure whose demand is sensitive to the growth of population in the household-formation age groups.

A longer-term effect of momentum is the very large increase in absolute population size that is projected to occur in developing regions during the next century. In population projections prepared at the World Bank, shown in table 2-3, global population is expected to increase by almost 3 billion people from 1992 to 2025, when total population will reach the 8.1 billion mark. More significant, however, is the growing divide between the population size of the more-industrial and the less-industrial world. Whereas by the year 2100, the population of the less-industrial world will have more than doubled (from about 4 billion to about 10 billion), the population growth in the more-industrial world will be comparatively negligible (around 165 million). Thus, whereas in 1990, four of every five people lived in the developing countries, in 2100 that ratio will be closer to ten out of every eleven people.

Projections of Future Population Growth

Demography is not destiny, however. Projections, especially longer-term forecasts, are based on extrapolations of trends in vital rates that may turn out to be inaccurate. Until the spread of HIV/AIDS, population projections generally assumed continued progress in reducing mortality, with life expectancy steadily approaching some assumed maximum. As HIV prevalence levels started to indicate that the disease was spreading rapidly, especially in some countries in Sub-Saharan Africa and Asia, population projections have been revised to take account of increased mortality resulting from AIDS. AIDS mortality is expected to lower life expectancy by several years in the most affected countries but is not likely to have an immediately large impact on population growth because of the long incubation period of HIV. The longer-run demographic impact will build slowly because the transmission rate of HIV is low compared to that of other diseases.

The most recent United Nations population projections have attempted to account for potential AIDS mortality (United Nations 1993a). Comparing projected population size for fifteen high-prevalence countries, the aggregated total population for the year 2005 is 310 million without accounting for AIDS and 298 million after accounting for AIDS mortality, a difference of 12 million persons. For Uganda (with a current population of 18 million), the 2005 projection is 29.2 million without AIDS and 27.8 million with it. Even without

Table 2-3.   Population Projections, by Geographic Region, 1990–2100
(millions)

Region	1990	2000	2025	2050	2100
World	5,266	6,116	8,127	9,587	10,970
Less-industrial countries	4,052	4,843	6,763	8,221	9,592
More-industrial countries	1,215	1,273	1,364	1,366	1,378
Africa	628	822	1,432	2,001	2,646
East Africa	274	362	651	938	1,285
West Africa	214	286	520	735	975
North Africa	140	174	261	328	386
America	715	821	1,047	1,178	1,267
Latin America and the Caribbean	435	512	686	804	883
North America	280	309	361	374	384
Asia	3,107	3,628	4,758	5,516	6,154
East and Southeast Asia	1,788	2,009	2,430	2,644	2,824
South Asia	1,186	1,444	2,038	2,484	2,847
Southwest Asia	133	175	290	388	483
Europe and former U.S.S.R.	790	814	851	850	859
Oceania	27	31	38	42	45

Source: Bos and others 1994.

actual population decline, the impact of HIV/AIDS is likely to be very serious in its effects on the working-age population. This impact is complicated by the fact that a high proportion of those who are infected will survive long enough to have children (many of whom will themselves be infected) but will *not* live long enough to raise those children to young adulthood, creating enormous burdens for relatives and other survivors.

The World Bank projections assume that the total fertility rate will stabilize at the replacement level of 2.1 births per woman. The experience of many developed countries in this century, however, has been a decline to below replacement during the 1930s, followed by a baby boom in the 1950s and a return to below replacement in the 1970s and 1980s. Recently, a few developed countries show increasing fertility once again. It is quite possible that when the demographic transition is completed in the developing world, similar mixed patterns could occur.

The main value of long-term projections is their demonstration of the long-lasting effects of population momentum. This, in turn, points to the im-

portance of current interventions to reduce fertility in order to offset the cu-
mulating effect of continued population growth and its inherent momentum
on population size in the future. The projections in table 2-3 are based on
country-by-country assessments of recent trends in fertility and mortality and
are applied to age-specific population estimates for each country. Bongaarts
(1994b) examines three causal factors underlying population growth and its
momentum and ways to achieve a total developing-country population below
the nearly 10 billion projected for 2100 (see figure 2-3) through actions that
deal with these causal factors. The calculations are for the developing world
as a whole, but they illustrate scenarios that apply both in large countries (India, Nigeria) and in small ones (Chad, Zambia) that face a doubling or more
of their populations as a result of momentum.

Unwanted pregnancies and the persistence of demand for large families
are the main reasons for high rates of population growth. According to Bongaarts, eliminating unwanted fertility would reduce total projected

**Figure 2-3.   Effects of Underlying Causes of Population Growth on Future
Projections of Population Size in the Developing World, 1995–2100**

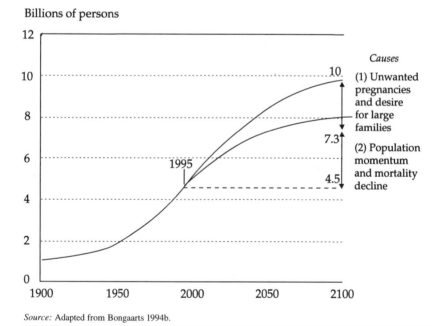

Billions of persons

Source: Adapted from Bongaarts 1994b.

developing-country population in 2100 from 10 to 8 billion, and motivating couples to have smaller families through increased investments in education and other social policy initiatives, especially those that lead to improvements in the status of women, could trim another 700 million from the projected total and lower the number to 7.3 billion.

Opinions differ about the relative weight of unwanted fertility and demand for large families in the persistence of fertility rates at levels above the replacement level (see chapter 4). But even if a combination of efforts on these two fronts were to reduce total fertility to replacement level, there still remains a projected 2.8 billion increase over and above the current population (around 4.5 billion) in developing countries attributable to population momentum and further declines in mortality. Although many demographers see population momentum as unalterable, it might be possible to reduce this figure. Delays in the timing of childbearing have an important impact on momentum. Later initiation of childbearing and longer intervals between births could cut momentum even if women continue to have two births during their childbearing years. A five-year delay in the mean age of childbearing would reduce the projected increase by 1 billion at the end of the next century.

The following chapters will examine in more detail the policy and program interventions to address high fertility and demographic momentum. The discussion will draw both on experience with family planning and reproductive health programs and on evidence about broader social policies that affect reproductive behavior.

Migration and Aging

Another important dimension of population is its changing geographic distribution. Only 17 percent of the population of developing countries was considered urban in 1950, but this had doubled to 34 percent in 1990. The projected population increase between 1990 and 2025 is almost entirely in urban areas, which include many of the world's "mega-cities," with populations of more than 10 million. According to the most recent United Nations projections, 57 percent of the population in developing countries will reside in urban areas by the year 2025 (United Nations 1993c).

A variety of forces has contributed to the increase in internal migration in developing countries. Natural increase has remained higher in rural areas, thereby increasing population pressures. Unequal distributions of land and agricultural production resources have forced many off the land, and attempts to increase production using more advanced agricultural technologies have made the agricultural sector less labor intensive. In some areas, for example the African Sahel, poor management of soil, water, and forest resources has further reduced the labor-absorptive capacity of rural areas. In situations of political instability, rural violence provides an added stimulus. On the "pull" side of the migration equation, potential migrants also perceive that there are greater job opportunities for themselves and educational opportunities for their children in urban areas. Improved transportation and communication have also fostered geographic mobility.

These same forces have stimulated flows of migrants across international borders. Historically, international migration provided an escape valve when European countries were experiencing population pressures during their demographic transitions. International migration has become increasingly important in the developing countries over the last two decades. Migration experts estimate that as of the mid-1980s approximately 100 million people were living outside their countries of birth or citizenship and that the numbers have undoubtedly increased in recent years. Accounting for migration flows is complicated by the presence of large numbers of undocumented persons, by the variety of types of movements, and by changes in international borders. The increase in international migration has important social, economic, and political significance for both sending and receiving countries.

Most of the recent attention to international migration has focused on movements from developing to industrial countries: from Mexico and Central America to the United States, from North Africa to Europe, and so forth. In fact, the greater share of international movers remains in the developing regions. By far the largest numbers are in Asia, the Middle East, and North Africa, which accounted for an estimated 35 million out of the global total. Migrants in Asia and in the Middle East and North Africa include many laborers in Persian Gulf states whose lives were disrupted by the 1991 Gulf War, as well as millions of Afghans, Palestinians, and other refugees from political upheavals. Many African movers are refugees from political violence (Mozambique, Somalia). But there are also significant movements of economic migrants (to South Africa and in West Africa). In Latin America and the Caribbean, both economic and political conditions have been factors in the movement of approximately 6 million people *within* the region, in addition to the estimated 13 million–15 million who had moved to the United States and Canada by the mid-1980s.

International population movements often have greater economic, social, and political impacts than purely demographic significance for both sending and receiving countries. Rising ethnic and racial tensions, other problems of integrating migrants in terms of language and culture, and recognition of the costs of providing social services for migrant workers and their dependents are creating a hostile climate that could make migration less attractive to potential movers. The migration process tends to be selective of better-trained, more ambitious workers, so that many potential employers oppose migration restrictions. Networks among migrants, once established, tend to encourage further movements. The benefits to sending countries can be substantial. Official remittances from migrant workers, estimated to be in excess of $70 billion in 1990, exceed official development assistance, estimated at $54 billion. Net official remittance flows to developing countries, which are far less than the total including unofficial flows, amounted to $37 billion in 1989, roughly 70 percent of official development assistance to those countries.

Population aging is another emerging issue. The global population aged sixty-five and over in 1990 is estimated to be 295 million. Although the percentages of those over sixty-five are highest in the developed world, developing countries are aging as well, as a result of declining fertility and mortality (see figure 2-4). It is also important to recognize that although the *percentages* of those over sixty-five are still low in developing areas, the *numbers* are already quite large and will become much larger during the next century. By the

Figure 2-4. Projected Growth, by Age Group, in Industrial and Developing Countries, 1990, 2025, and 2100

Billions of persons

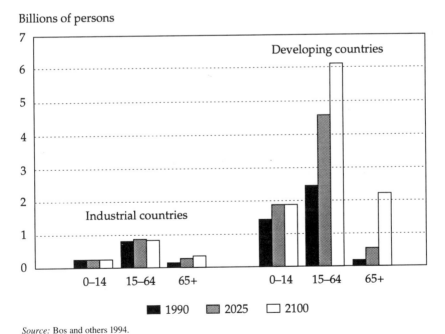

Source: Bos and others 1994.

end of that century, the number of people over age sixty-five in the developing areas will be greater than the number under age fifteen.

Aging might therefore be seen as the outcome of a success story. Given the dependency and health needs of the elderly population, however, it is not without consequences for social expenditures. In Europe, the oldest region, 14 percent of the population is currently sixty-five years of age and over; this is projected to increase to 22 percent in 2025. Although developing countries have more time before their populations reach such levels, the population aging process will occur more rapidly than in Europe and other areas whose demographic transitions took longer. For developing countries now moving rapidly through those transitions, the capacity to support an aging population will depend on investments in the human resource potential of the current generation of youth, who will be the first to experience the increased pressures of dependency at the upper end of the age distribution.

The rapid urbanization of the population, international migration, and population aging are important aspects of the population equation in developing countries. Traditionally, demographers have dealt mainly with issues of population growth rates and fertility rates. Now other aspects of the population picture require more attention, and governments are already striving to develop policies that deal not only with the increased numbers of people in their countries but also with the age and geographical redistribution of their populations. The report returns to these questions and how the Bank should address them during the discussion of operational issues in chapter 7.

Note

1. The amount of momentum in Asian countries with large population bases is striking. China, where fertility is now at replacement level, will add another 200 million–300 million to its current 1.1 billion population as a result of momentum. India, where fertility is currently higher than in China, is expected to pass China in total population size as a result of momentum. Because of India's large and youthful population base, a fifteen-year delay in reaching replacement fertility translates into a difference of more than half a billion persons by the time the growth rate slows down at the end of the next century (Haub 1992).

CHAPTER THREE

Rationales for Public Sector Involvement in Population

BORROWERS, the Bank, and other donors have been involved in population activities for two reasons. The first is concern that rapid population growth will impede efforts to raise living standards, particularly in poor countries. The second is the belief that lower fertility will bring health and welfare benefits to individuals and families in those countries. There have been two main rationales to justify the role of public policy in these areas: (1) the existence of *externalities* in fertility decisions, that is, in their childbearing decisions parents do not take into account the effects on others of these choices, and (2) failures in the markets for reproductive health and family planning services per se, because individuals may have *imperfect information* about the possible methods of fertility regulation or about the health benefits of spacing and family limitation. This chapter reviews the analytical and empirical bases for these arguments.

Externalities: Societal Effects of Rapid Population Growth

The externalities rationale for public sector involvement in population hinges on the argument that there are adverse effects of rapid population growth resulting from gaps between individual and family perceptions of the benefits and costs of childbearing decisions and the actual public costs of these actions. These gaps occur for many reasons (see Chomitz and Birdsall 1991). All families value children; however, the poor may have added reasons for wanting large families. Private benefits may be exceeded by the social costs of educating and employing children, particularly in transitional situations in which new skills are needed for the next generation to support itself. The strength of the externalities argument depends primarily on the extent to which population growth has negative effects on efforts to achieve economic growth, reduce poverty (particularly through investments in human resources), and preserve the environment in poor countries.

Most of the debate has focused on the effects of population growth rates. However, population size and distribution are also relevant, particularly for environmental issues. Exactly what the consequences will be as populations in developing countries rapidly double their current size is a matter of disagreement among experts. Debate continues between those who note that pessimistic prognoses cannot be proved and those who argue that efforts to develop human capital and manage environmental resources would be easier if population grew less rapidly and if, by speeding up the transition to lower fertility, the projected increases in total population size associated with demographic momentum could be offset through policy measures suggested in the previous chapter.

Population and Economic Growth

Attempts to demonstrate consistent cross-national macroeconomic effects of high rates of population growth have, for the most part, been inconclusive. Although it has been possible to demonstrate *potential* adverse effects of rapid population growth with illustrative mathematical models linking demographic and macroeconomic changes, efforts to measure the adverse effects of rapid population growth with cross-national data provide only limited support for that argument. A recent review (Kelley and Schmidt 1994) of a wide range of models linking the rate of population growth to two measures—per capita output growth and per worker productivity—reached the following conclusions about these effects.

- They are not statistically significant in the 1960s or 1970s, a finding consistent with a wide literature.
- They are statistically significant and quantitatively large in the 1980s.
- They vary with the level of economic development, being negative in poorer countries and sometimes positive for more-industrial countries.

Similar findings emerge when the analysis is focused on the impact of the high youth-dependency rates on savings in developing countries. Relatively weak impacts are found for the 1960s and 1970s; however, the dependency-rate impact on savings for the 1980s is sufficiently large to account, at least in part, for the negative impact of population growth on the growth of per capita output in poor countries.

Such cross-national assessments need to be interpreted with considerable caution. They are, at most, indicative of linkages at the country level, which need to be assessed in relation to the specific experiences of those countries. The data themselves are subject to many limitations, and the causal chains linking demographic changes to development problems are often quite complex. The U.S. National Academy of Sciences report on the adverse effects of rapid population growth (National Research Council 1986) highlighted the mediating role that institutional factors and governance capacity play in these relationships, noting, for example, that the strengths and weaknesses of financial and administrative institutions in developing countries need to be recognized in assessing negative age-dependency effects of rapid population growth on savings rates in poor countries. The erosive effect of population pressures on administrative reforms and efforts to improve public management has also been recognized, but this too has proven hard to quantify.

Although cross-national studies do not show that population growth slows economic growth in all countries, they do suggest that rapid growth (above 2 percent a year) inhibits efforts to raise incomes in poor countries with high fertility and youthful age distributions. This is illustrated in country-level studies. For example, a World Bank review of human resource needs in Malawi noted that the labor force is expected to double between 1990 and 2010 and that the agricultural sector is already hard-pressed to absorb additional labor. The report concluded that without declines in fertility, it would be unlikely that the country could increase the amount of capital per worker enough to produce significant improvements in productivity, wages, and living standards in the foreseeable future (World Bank 1992a). Similar conclusions have been reached for other countries in Sub-Saharan Africa. An example from another region, South Asia, is the Bank's review of the consequences of rapid population growth in Pakistan, which covered a range of development objectives, including human resource investments and employment. The report concluded that the costs of continued high fertility fall heaviest on the most vulnerable members of society—women, children, and the poor—and called for broad-based efforts to reduce the high fertility rates still prevalent in that country (World Bank 1989).

Population and Poverty Reduction

Most of the rapid increase in population over the last forty years has occurred in the poorest of the less-industrial countries. Recent assessments indicate that the incidence of absolute poverty in the developing world as a whole remained static during the 1980s, with one in three persons consuming less than $1 of goods per day. The number of poor has been growing at the same rate as the aggregate population of the developing world, about 2 percent a year, with generally rising incidence in Africa and Latin America and falling incidence in Asia (Chen, Datt, and Ravallion 1993).

The anticipated increase in the world's poor populations can also be seen in table 3-1, which shows the global distribution of population among countries of different economic status. Most of the population increase is concentrated in low-income countries. Two-thirds of the 1.3 billion people being added to global population between 1985 and 2000 will reside in currently poor countries. Between 1985 and 2025, people in low-income countries (average 1990 per capita income: $350) are projected to increase from 57 percent to 61 percent of the world's total. Over the same period, the proportion of those in the high-income countries (average 1990 per capita income: $19,590) will fall, from 16 percent in 1985 to 11 percent in 2025.

Despite the high correlation between rapid population growth and poverty, analyses of cross-national research have found little evidence that population growth in and of itself causes poverty. Rather, the evidence suggests that the relationships are complex and that high fertility is as much a symptom of poverty as a cause. Ahlburg (1994) found little evidence of a direct link

Table 3-1. **Population Projections, by Income Group, 1985–2025**
(millions)

Region	1985	2000	2025
World	5,266	6,116	8,127
Less-industrial countries	4,052	4,843	6,763
More-industrial countries	1,215	1,273	1,364
Income group in 1990			
Low	3,072	3,653	5,062
Lower middle	914	1,057	1,425
Upper middle	463	540	718
High	817	865	922

Source: Bos and others 1994.

between population growth and poverty levels in a multicountry analysis. Ahlburg suggests that population growth may affect poverty indirectly, either through its negative impact on the growth of per capita income in the poorest countries, as argued above, or through its effect on the provision of education and other social services, or directly through the size and structure of families.

Within countries, rapid population growth can also hinder efforts to reduce the incidence of poverty, through the inhibiting effect of continually increasing numbers on the effort to expand access and improve the quality of education, health, and other human services and through the self-perpetuating cycle of high fertility and low income in poor households. Again, the relationships are complex, and explorations of cross-national evidence show little direct link between a rapid increase in numbers and deterioration in the quality of education, for example. In fact, effective public sector management turns out to be more important than population per se. As Kelley (1994: 27–28) has noted, "A major impact of population growth has been to reveal the consequences of bad policies sooner and more dramatically; as such, population growth 'exacerbates' some problems but may not be their most important cause." He goes on to caution against raising the expectation that slowing population growth will solve such problems, arguing instead that the most defensible strategy is one that advances an appropriate balance between direct efforts in the affected sector and population policy.

When human resource and population policies are mutually reinforcing, the effects can be striking. For example, in their study of the extraordinary expansion of education in the so-called "East Asian Miracle" countries, Birdsall and Sabot (1993; see also World Bank 1993a) found strong, positively reinforcing relationships between human resource investments, positive macroeconomic policies, and early completion of the demographic transition. In contrast, where policies are not complementary, the mutual interactions between rapid population growth, poor government policy, and poverty lead in a negative rather than a positive direction. This was the situation found by Tan and Mingat (1992) in a broader sample of Asian countries, including several with high rates of population growth, questionable economic policies, and inefficient educational policies.

Other effects of high fertility on individual welfare are apparent in comparisons of households classified by per capita income in Brazil, Colombia, Malaysia, and rural India. The ratio of income per child in the richest households to that in the poorest in the 1970s ranged from about 12:1 in rural India to more than 100:1 in Brazil. Studies that compared data from the 1970s and the early 1990s show that the decline in fertility in Malaysia was accompanied by a closing of the gap in per child resources between the lowest and highest quintiles of families. A study of twins in India found that the additional unexpected child reduced school enrollment levels of all children in households with twins (see Rosenzweig and Schultz 1985).

Research on the intra-household allocation of resources finds less investment in children in larger families, particularly in societies that are at the initial stages of their demographic transition process (when mortality is declining but fertility remains high or is rising; see Lloyd 1993). Patterns vary according to cultural and social contexts. Where there is strong preference for sons, the adverse effects are likely to be worse for girls. In many parts of the world, parents with more children tend to discriminate more strongly against female children in the allocation of schooling and other forms of investment than parents with fewer children. When these girls reach adulthood, they will have been socialized to perform more traditional roles and will be less likely to regulate their fertility and therefore more likely to perpetuate the cycle of poverty and large family size.

The story that emerges from evidence about societal-level effects of population growth does not support the neo-Malthusian view that population growth is the root cause of all development problems. Nonetheless, it suggests that efforts to reduce high growth rates are worth pursuing in poor countries where rapid growth impedes human resource investments and poverty reduction. The linkages between population growth and these goals are complex and vary in their nature and severity. Most of the impact is mediated through effects on other variables that affect human resource investments at both the societal and household levels, where large numbers erode or impede the quality of those investments. Slowing of population growth will not, by itself, reduce poverty; nor is it a substitute for sound macroeconomic and sectoral policies. It can buy time to do the things that are necessary to achieve other key development objectives, however, and it will reduce the pressures on budgets and administrative structures that make their achievement so difficult in the poorest countries.

Population and the Environment

The question of how population growth affects the long-term sustainability of development efforts gained prominence during preparations for the 1992 United Nations Conference on Environment and Development in Rio de Janeiro, Brazil. A key concern was whether efforts to feed and employ the very large increments in population that are being projected for poor countries will contribute to environmental degradation and undermine efforts to manage resources on a sustainable basis. The views range from optimistic to pessimistic. Economists have been generally optimistic about some environmental issues that in the past were cited as reasons to "do something" about population growth. Their views are based on the expectation that markets and the price mechanism will induce changes in resource use and call forth alternative inputs and techniques that keep economic systems in balance.

With qualifications—some of major significance, as in rural Sub-Saharan Africa—economists believe that the market can address the interaction of population and environment. This view is reflected in the 1986 National Academy of Sciences report that concluded, "The scarcity of exhaustible resources is at most a minor constraint on economic growth in the near to intermediate term" (National Research Council 1986: 16). Others are not so sanguine. The report that emanated from the 1993 scientific summit meeting in New Delhi, representing the opinions of fifty-seven scientific academies, noted, "The academies believe that ultimate success in dealing with global social, economic, and environmental problems cannot be achieved without a stable world population" (World Scientific Academies 1993).

In Africa, the Bank's study on linkages between population and environmental degradation illustrates how the market can break down (Cleaver and Schreiber 1993). It cites evidence on how the pressure of population growth has eliminated the central element—the ability to move freely on the land—that has enabled pastoralists to derive their livelihood in a sustainable manner from the natural resource endowment of their environment (see box 3-1). Rapid population growth has narrowed the scope for further expansion of production, and new cultivation techniques have not been introduced fast enough to prevent soil erosion and declining yields. Much of rural Africa today is facing overgrazing, deforestation, depletion of water resources, and loss of natural habitat.

The focus of the ongoing debate about population and food supply has also shifted toward environmental issues (see Bongaarts 1994a). Advances in food-production technology and better policies have made it possible to expand global food production faster than population over the past two decades. These increases occurred in Asia and Latin America, but not Africa, where per capita production declined. Even in Africa, the potential for increased food production is quite large. However, environmentalists are concerned that the technologies required for increased production will damage the environment by increasing soil erosion and depleting water tables. Careful management can avoid such risks, but poor countries with high rates of population growth and other pressures may not be willing or able to pay the costs of adopting sustainable approaches to increased food production.

Soil and water resources are examples of renewable common-property resources, which are subject to excessive exploitation, pollution, and degradation. Analysts have found that slower population growth might allow more time for developing countries to implement the policies and to develop the

BOX 3-1. THE POPULATION-
AGRICULTURE-ENVIRONMENT NEXUS
IN SUB-SAHARAN AFRICA

Shifting cultivation and grazing have
been appropriate traditional responses to abundant land, scarce capital, and limited technology. As population densities grew slowly during the
first half of this century, these extensive systems evolved into more intensive systems, as in Rwanda, Burundi,
the Kenyan highlands, and the Kivu
Plateau in Zaire. This slowly evolving
system has proved unable, however,
to adapt to sharply accelerated population growth over the past four decades. Traditional uses of land and
fuel have depleted soil and forests and
contributed to agricultural stagnation.
Stagnant incomes and the absence of
improvements in human resources
have impeded the demographic transi-

tion. A combination of high population
densities and low investment has
caused arable land per person to decline from 0.5 hectare in 1965 to 0.3
hectare in 1987. As a result, in many
parts of Burundi, Kenya, Lesotho, Li-
beria, Mauritania, and Rwanda fallow
periods are no longer sufficient to re-
store fertility.

Population growth drives some people to cultivate land not previously
used for farming: for example, in semi-
arid areas and in tropical forests,
where soil and climatic conditions are
poorly suited for annual cropping or for
the practices employed by the new migrants. These problems are most severe in parts of the Sahel, in parts of
mountainous East Africa, and in the
dry belt stretching from Namibia
through Botswana, Lesotho, and
southern Mozambique.

Source: World Bank 1992c.

institutions necessary to protect the environment. Economists tend to be more
optimistic about creating market capacity to balance long-run costs and benefits than environmentalists, who argue that population increase has been out-
running the adaptation process and warn of systemic breakdowns once certain
"no-return" thresholds are crossed.

With the exception of trends such as global warming, linkages between
population, environmental degradation, and management of natural resources
tend to be regional and local rather than global in expression, although examples exist of situations in which human activities in one place contribute to
environmental problems in another. Such environmental problems as air and
water pollution are virtually inevitable wherever human beings congregate in
large numbers, suggesting that problems will become even more of a challenge in the future as urbanization continues and urban areas grow in population and size. The influence of population on problems of air, water, and land
management occurs through its interactions with such factors as technology,
consumption levels, and social organization.

In dealing with specific environmental problems associated with population, the time frame for planning and policy actions becomes an important issue. Because of population momentum, the relatively near-term benefits of acting on population in such areas as air or water quality or safe water supply and sanitation may be small. In the long run, however, achievable reductions in population growth could make substantial differences in one multiplier of environmental impacts: human population size.

To be sure, many uncertainties remain about long-term population growth in developing countries: its magnitude, its geographic distribution, and the severity of its environmental impacts. The risks of adverse environmental consequences associated with continued rapid growth of population in poor areas are serious enough, however, to warrant action to slow population growth as quickly as possible. Moreover, the existing poverty and weak institutional capacity of governments in many of these areas raise serious questions as to whether those governments will be successful in implementing the institutional and technological changes needed to manage large increases in population without further damage to their countries' environments.

In the face of these uncertainties and the risks associated with failing to make the adjustments needed to accommodate very large increases in population in poor areas, an argument can be made for application of the "precautionary principle," which suggests the prudent reduction of risks where possible. Although it is virtually impossible to estimate what the potential carrying capacity of such areas will be for human activity, it is certain that they will not have indefinite capacity to support large additions of people. The prudent course, then, would surely be *not* to test the environment's vulnerability, elasticity, and recoupability to the outer limits: once the damage is done, it probably cannot be repaired, and the adverse effects on the health and well-being of affected populations are likely to be great. In the case of population, the precautionary principle suggests that feasible policy actions to reduce population growth and offset the long-term effects of demographic momentum are worthwhile. The same principle applies to improving technology, reducing wasteful consumption, and otherwise conserving natural resources.

Individual Reproductive Health and Welfare

The rationale for government action in reproductive health and family planning does not end with the negative consequences of population growth. Even in country circumstances where rapid population growth is not a concern, public sector involvement in reproductive health and family planning is warranted. The timing and spacing of pregnancies and the degree to which they are wanted, independent of their total number, have important impacts on maternal and child health. This health impact on women and their families, combined with failures in the markets for health and fertility regulation, provides an impetus for public action even where demographic concerns are absent and can be an equally, if not more, compelling reason for those actions when demographic concerns are present.

High Fertility and Reproductive Health

Studies are providing increasingly strong evidence of the negative consequences of badly timed or unwanted fertility on family well-being. The adverse health consequences of pregnancies that are too closely spaced or that occur too early or too late in the reproductive life cycle are documented in *World Development Report 1993* (World Bank 1993e). Enabling women and men to exercise better control over their reproductive lives therefore brings both individual and societal health and welfare benefits. These benefits involve more than just the avoidance of sickness and disease. Proper timing and spacing of births enable mothers to take better care of themselves, their children, and other family members. Poorly timed and inadequately spaced births increase the risk of morbidity and mortality for both mothers and children. They are also an increased burden on the health care system and draw resources away from other uses. Three areas where reproductive health outcomes could be improved warrant specific attention: avoiding high-risk pregnancies, reducing maternal and child mortality and morbidity, and reducing health risks in fertility regulation.

Avoiding High-Risk Pregnancies

Pregnancy and birth always carry some risks for the mother and child; but some pregnancies have predictably higher risks for mothers and children than others. By avoiding such high-risk pregnancies, maternal and child health can be improved.[1] Pregnancies that occur too early or too late in a woman's reproductive life, that are too closely spaced, that occur to women who have already had many births, that occur to women who have health problems such as high blood pressure and diabetes that could be aggravated by pregnancy, and that are unwanted all pose health risks for mothers and/or for their children. Unwanted pregnancies are a matter of health risk for all women, particularly when unwanted pregnancies lead to unsafe abortions. The avoidance of unwanted pregnancy protects women from exposure to these risks. Quantifying these risks and the number of abortion-related deaths and injuries is extremely difficult because in most countries of the developing world, abortion is illegal and is not reported by the person who performs it, the woman, or her family.

Reducing Infant and Child Mortality

The factors that cause higher risk for infants and children are somewhat different from those that cause higher maternal mortality. Births to older women and high-parity births are less likely to elevate the risk for the child than to elevate the risk for the mother, while births to very young women bring high risks to both mother and child. Closely spaced births are more likely to affect the survival chances of the child than of the mother. However, a mother's death from complications of pregnancy and labor is almost always associated with the death of her infant. An estimated 7 million perinatal infant deaths annually are associated with poor maternal health and poor management of pregnancies (see Tinker and Koblinsky 1993).

Reducing Maternal Mortality and Morbidity

Few data exist on maternal mortality in developing countries. Therefore, one must consider the relative risks reported as rough approximations. In high-fertility countries, however, a woman is at risk of pregnancy-related mortality many times during her reproductive lifetime. Each year, an estimated 500,000 maternal deaths occur in the developing world. For each of those deaths, there are, in addition, between ten and sixteen cases of maternal morbidity. Data from India indicate that women have a higher risk of dying between the ages of fifteen and forty-nine than men and that this risk is due primarily to the health risks of childbearing. To put these mortality differences in broader perspective, it has been estimated that in high-fertility areas of West and Central Africa women have a 1-in-20 chance of dying from maternal causes, while in low-fertility East Asia, women have a 1-in-722 chance of maternal death. In North Europe, with its somewhat lower fertility and much better health facilities, the chances are 1 in 10,000 (Tinker and Koblinsky 1993). The World Health Organization estimates that in half of the developing countries, maternal mortality is the first or second most common cause of death among women twenty-five to thirty-four years old. In all others, it is in the top ten (see Winikoff 1987).

The risks of maternal death depend on both age and parity. Girls who bear a child before age eighteen are three times more likely to die in childbirth than women who bear their first child between the ages of twenty and twenty-nine. First births are generally more risky than second or third births, but as parity rises over three, the risk of maternal mortality tends to increase. There is a debate in the literature about whether high mortality of mothers under eighteen and their infants is the result of young age, primiparous status, or the fact that women who bear children early tend to be from poorer families and receive less health care and poorer nutrition. Some researchers suggest that the higher risks of early childbearing are related to physiological factors such as smaller pelvises (particularly under age sixteen), pregnancy-induced hypertension, and more frequent pregnancy-aggravated malaria; this evidence has not clarified whether it is age per se or poverty and lack of medical care that is most important in contributing to these hazards (National Research Council 1989). Depending on the ages and reproductive intentions of expectant mothers, adequate timing, spacing, or limiting of pregnancies could help reduce such risks. Many women in developing countries say they want to space or limit their births but are not doing so. Others are at risk and do not express a desire to limit or space births but might do so if they received adequate counseling about the health risks of a poorly timed pregnancy.

Reducing Health Risk in Fertility Regulation

Risk is attached not only to pregnancy but also to a lesser extent to the use of methods to prevent births. Survey data point to a considerable scope for providing family planning information and services to women who want to space or limit births. In some cases, women do not have access to the temporary methods appropriate for spacing; others may use temporary methods, but because of inadequate information use them poorly, resulting in method failure or discontinuation. The quality of family planning services is, in many instances, inadequate for women who want to space their children. In other instances, women do not have access to permanent methods and are exposed to long periods of failure with temporary methods because method mix is limited, providers are not trained to recognize and respond to health problems and other client concerns, or counseling about side effects and follow-up with problems that arise are inadequate.

Thus adequate information and methods of fertility regulation are crucial to achieving and maintaining reproductive health and provide two rationales for public involvement in reproductive health and family planning services. First, without public action, the market will not provide sufficient information about the health consequences of fertility patterns and fertility regulation methods. Second, many governments may decide that contraception is a good to which all are entitled, and therefore undertake to provide it to persons whom the market would ignore. These arguments about the role of the public sector parallel those in *World Development Report 1993*, which recommends that reproductive health and family planning services be included in preventive health services.

Standard economic analyses assume that people have access to full information relevant to their decisions. In the case of reproductive health and family planning, this requires that women be able to know the consequences of childbearing and child spacing for their own and their children's health and that they be aware of the relevant characteristics (safety, efficacy, convenience) of fertility regulation methods. When such assumptions do not hold, there is scope for government to provide information on efficiency grounds. Information takes on characteristics of a public good similar to other preventive health measures. Access to it cannot be limited to those willing to pay for it, and hence it will be underprovided by the private economy, if provided at all.

Examples of market failures that deprive underserved groups of the health and welfare benefits of choice and control over reproduction include cases where fertility regulation methods requiring medical backup (intrauterine devices or surgical sterilization) are not provided, where private health services are not accessible to the poor, or where health infrastructure is generally lacking. Lack of information is frequently cited as a reason for high-risk pregnancies (see chapter 4). Although surveys report that most interviewees can name at least one method of contraception, in-depth analyses reveal that few understand the side effects or how to use methods correctly, indicating that counseling is inadequate. One consequence of this is that even when contraceptives are commercially available, contraceptive failure rates are high and involve serious health consequences. These limitations in the market for contraceptive information and services show up in a higher incidence of high-risk pregnancies for poorer, less educated women even in countries that have higher average levels of contraceptive prevalence.

Public Sector Action Is Warranted

The rationales for public sector action to speed up the transition to lower fertility in poor countries are strongest with respect to failure in the market for reproductive health/family planning information and services. Corrective action is important for human development and poverty reduction and also contributes to lower rates of population growth. Societal-level evidence about externalities resulting from the adverse effects of rapid population growth is problematic and does not support across-the-board generalizations about the adverse effects of population growth that once characterized the population debate. Nevertheless, public sector actions to slow high rates of population growth are also warranted in poor countries where population growth hampers efforts to invest in human resources, reduce poverty, and protect the environment.

These rationales apply for government involvement in reproductive health/family planning as well as broader social policy aimed at speeding up fertility declines through increasing educational opportunities, particularly for girls, raising the status of women, reducing poverty, and achieving economic growth. Such policies are justified in their own right on welfare grounds similar to the ones outlined above for reproductive health and family planning, but they may be supported for the added and often powerful impact that they have in reducing the demand for large families and motivating the practice of fertility regulation. In most instances, interventions justified on the basis of societal objectives also serve individual interests. Where they are in actual or potential conflict—as in the case of concerns registered by reproductive rights advocates about population policies that put heavy weight on slowing population growth—consideration needs to be given to ways in which individual and societal interests and responsibilities can be harmonized.

The next chapter identifies a broad range of channels through which public policy could influence fertility. The following two chapters discuss specific options in terms of social policies affecting fertility (chapter 5) and interventions in the market for reproductive health and family planning information and services (chapter 6).

Note

1. Reproductive health risks are not limited to high-risk groups. In fact, most maternal deaths occur outside these groups, even though the relative risk is less. Lower fertility can also affect the *numbers* of maternal deaths by reducing the numbers exposed to the overall risk associated with pregnancy.

CHAPTER FOUR

Demand and Supply Factors in Fertility Transitions

$\mathbf{F}$EW social changes are as well documented as the fertility declines now occurring in developing countries. Starting with data from the World Fertility Survey twenty years ago and continuing with information from the most recent round of Demographic and Health Surveys, along with a variety of related survey efforts, demographers have been able to track trends in fertility over the three decades in which these declines have been under way. In addition to information on fertility rates, these surveys shed light on the practice of fertility regulation and on the social and economic characteristics associated with changes in reproductive behavior.

The Demand for Children

High fertility reflects cultural and social norms supportive of larger families as well as high levels of infant and child mortality that require additional births to ensure that the desired number of children survive to adulthood. The costs of child rearing are low in such settings; these include both direct costs (food, clothing, housing, and others) as well as indirect or opportunity costs such as the time that mothers or older sisters devote to child care. Benefits of large families include added labor, particularly in rural settings, support for parents in old age, as well as other claims or entitlements (for example, to land holdings) based on the number of individuals in a household. Regulation of fertility is subject to social control, for example, through customs that determine when, whom, and even whether individuals can marry and bear children and through traditional practices such as postpartum abstinence, separation of spouses, and breast-feeding. In addition to its direct purpose of nourishing newborns, breast-feeding may or may not be intended as a means of spacing births.

Demand theories of fertility decline focus on changes in the balance of costs and benefits of children and on how shifts in this balance relate to changes in the costs of fertility regulation. The reason why fertility decline has generally accompanied economic growth and social development is that those processes induce shifts in the balance of the cost-benefit ratio for children. Some of these shifts are by-products of other changes associated with social and economic structure—for example, migration from rural to urban areas, which raises the cost of housing or breaks down traditional mechanisms for support of parents in old age as part of familial inheritance arrangements. Others may be the result of public policies that may or may not have explicit population objectives—for example, compulsory education, which reduces the labor value of children and raises their costs through school fees, books, clothing, and transportation. As is explained in the next section, education also affects the demand for children by affecting reproductive attitudes and by increasing the value of women's time and thus raising the opportunity costs of child rearing.

The links to costs of fertility regulation can be addressed as they relate to the rising costs of children. If means of fertility regulation are not available or are obtainable only at very high monetary or opportunity cost (for example, having to travel a long distance to obtain them) or at high psychological or human cost (for example, the practice of infanticide or unsafe abortion), there will be very little fertility control as long as the number of births and desired fertility are in balance. As social, economic, and demographic changes (mortality decline) reduce the desire or need for a large number of births, the proportion of unwanted pregnancies will increase, and eventually the costs associated with unwanted fertility will rise to levels that motivate individuals to incur the costs of fertility regulation. If the development of private markets for contraceptives accompanies the economic and social changes that raise the costs of children, the practice of fertility regulation will reduce unwanted pregnancies and lead to fertility decline (as it did in the industrial countries). The same could occur if externalities associated with rapid population growth or failures in markets for fertility regulation lead governments to provide contraceptive information or services. Both would influence fertility by reducing the costs, monetary as well as psychological, of regulating fertility relative to the costs of incurring unwanted pregnancy.

The experiences of a number of developing countries that have experienced rapid fertility transitions over the last two decades indicate that the demand for fertility regulation increases fairly rapidly when social and economic conditions are undergoing rapid change. Potential consumers have demonstrated their willingness to use contraceptives when private markets or government programs offer high-quality services that respond to their needs. Experience has also shown that these needs involve more than mere access to contraceptives, which account for only a small portion of the total array of information and services that consumers desire. In the case of resupply methods, contraceptives generally can be procured through pharmacies and commercial outlets once client relationships have been established. The effectiveness of services in helping clients to realize their reproductive aspirations, including better spacing or limiting of pregnancies, has generally depended on the quality as well as the location and cost of services being provided. In many cases, even very poor clients have shown that they are willing to pay for services that respond to their needs and that they will not use free services that do not address those needs.

Demand and Supply Issues

A key question for population policy in countries in South Asia and other regions that have not yet completed their transitions to lower fertility is whether efforts to expand the family planning services that played an important role in getting fertility declines under way will be sufficient to finish the transition to low fertility or whether greater attention needs to be given to underlying social and economic conditions as transitions reach an intermediate stage. This question is also relevant for countries at an early stage in their fertility transition, which may learn from the experiences of countries that have already completed that stage. The issue is particularly important for low-income countries in Sub-Saharan Africa, which lack much of the social and health infrastructure that aided fertility declines in Asia and Latin America once contraceptives became more widely available through organized family planning programs and through private and commercial channels.

Debate about the relative importance of the supply of contraception and factors affecting the demand for children in fertility transitions has waxed and waned for more than two decades. When efforts to expand family planning were just getting under way in developing countries during the early 1970s, there was considerable skepticism about whether demand for contraception would be sufficient to bring significant change in reproductive behavior. "Development is the best contraceptive" was a catchphrase at the 1974 World Population Conference in Bucharest, with a bottom-line recommendation that fertility would decline faster if spending were shifted from family planning programs to changing the underlying social structure that generated demand for large families. This view was supported by a strong body of evidence on the linkages between fertility decline and educational attainment, improvements in the economic and social status of women, and other factors such as urbanization and the spread of mass communications.

When the supply-demand debate was most intense during the 1970s, supply was fairly narrowly defined in terms of the availability of contraceptives. As program experience has deepened and been evaluated, the definition of supply has broadened to address a range of information and services that family planning programs provide to help clients realize their reproductive aspirations. Recognizing this, many family planning programs have invested in information, education, and communication efforts aimed at informing potential clients about the benefits of spacing and limiting births and about how to use fertility regulation methods effectively. Many programs have used the media to raise consciousness about family planning and to motivate couples to space and limit births. Even the nonspecific content of mass media messages, particularly those that expose audiences to new values and the concept of choice, can play an important role in this process. Although these influences are difficult to quantify, they are recognized as playing an important role in strengthening motivation for family planning (see Church 1989; Gilluly and Moore 1986).

These efforts to influence fertility preferences and attitudes toward family planning have often proved to be as important as the actual provision of contraceptives. They have generally been labeled as "demand creation." However, it is important not to equate this use of the term with its broader use in the supply-demand context discussed above. Both senses of demand are important for understanding reproductive behavior, but the first refers specifically to efforts to motivate the practice of fertility regulation for purposes of either limiting or spacing births, while the second encompasses the effects of a broad range of social and economic changes that shape reproductive attitudes and practices.

The Pivotal Role of Education

Much of the debate about the relative importance of supply-and-demand factors in family planning has focused on whether investments in female education or funding of family planning programs would be more effective in accelerating fertility declines in developing countries. As Cochrane (1979: 29) has demonstrated, the effects of an individual's education on fertility are likely to work through multiple channels: "Education through literacy gives people access to more sources of information and a wider perspective on their own culture. Education is also a socializing process and inculcates social values. Exposure to these values would depend on the years of schooling. Education is widely believed to provide economic skills, and the level of those skills may depend on the grade level attended. Even if education does not provide such skills, jobs are often rationed on the basis of credentials such as education certificates." Improved educational opportunities and higher returns to schooling can also induce parents to have fewer children and invest more in each child.

That schooling has a powerful effect on reproductive behavior is undisputed. Data from the Demographic and Health Surveys reveal the same consistent correlation between fertility and educational attainment, both between and within countries, that has been observed in numerous earlier inquiries. Table 4-1 summarizes evidence assembled from those surveys in a forthcoming United Nations review of linkages between women's education and fertility (United Nations forthcoming). At the individual level, the table shows differences of two to five births between women with no education and those with ten or more years of schooling. The importance of education for fertility decline is also underscored in numerous cross-national analyses that have examined its direct effect (see Subbarao and Raney 1993) or its indirect influence, for example, by shaping reproductive aspirations (see Pritchett 1994).

Survey data demonstrate the effect of educational attainment on three important behaviors related to fertility: age at marriage, duration of breast-feeding, and contraceptive use. Schultz (1994) has compiled data on these relationships from the World Fertility Survey; they are reported in table 4-2. These data reveal a three- to five-year differential in the average age at marriage between women with no education and those with seven or more years of schooling. This is very significant with respect to the population momentum issue raised in chapter 2, where it is shown that a five-year delay in the average age of childbearing (which is closely correlated with age at marriage) could reduce by as much as 1 billion the total population in standard projections for the developing countries in the next century.

The data also reveal one of the challenges faced by family planning programs in reducing fertility at the early stages of the transition process: the tendency for the average duration of breast feeding (and the corresponding period of postpartum amenorrhea) to decrease with the years of schooling. Part of the effect of increased contraceptive use on fertility is offset by this decrease in the other proximate determinant of fertility. For this reason, family planning programs have stepped up their emphasis on continuing the practice of breast-feeding, which in addition to its health benefits for infants also has a natural contraceptive effect if practiced exclusively.

Large percentages of women with no schooling and low literacy have

Table 4-1. Fertility Rates, by Women's Years of Education and Region

Region	Mean years of education	Total	Years of education 0	1–3	4–6	7–9	10+	Difference between 10+ and 0
Sub-Saharan Africa								
Botswana	5.5	5.0	5.9	5.6	5.1	4.5	3.1	−2.8
Burundi	0.9	7.0	7.0	7.4	6.7	(6.6)	(4.2)	−2.8
Ghana	4.9	6.4	7.1	6.6	6.4	6.8	4.9	−2.2
Kenya	5.2	6.7	7.2	7.5	7.5	6.2	4.6	−2.6
Liberia	2.6	6.6	6.8	7.1	7.5	5.7	4.2	−2.6
Mali	0.9	6.9	7.0	6.9	6.6	5.7	(4.7)	−2.3
Senegal	1.5	6.6	7.0	6.4	5.5	4.3	3.6	−3.4
Togo	2.3	6.6	7.2	7.1	6.0	3.9	4.8	−2.4
Uganda	3.3	7.3	7.7	7.4	7.0	7.2	5.3	−2.4
Zimbabwe	6.0	5.7	7.3	7.2	6.3	5.0	3.3	−4.0
Northern Africa[a]								
Egypt	3.1	4.7	5.7	5.3	4.2	3.4	3.4	−2.3
Morocco	1.1	4.9	5.5	3.9	2.9	2.4	2.2	−3.3
Tunisia	2.8	4.4	5.1	4.7	3.7	2.8	2.6	−2.5
Asia[a]								
Indonesia	4.3	3.4	3.8	4.0	3.6	2.8	2.6	−1.2
Sri Lanka	6.3	2.8	2.8	3.0	2.9	2.7	2.7	−0.1
Thailand	4.8	2.4	3.5	2.8	2.5	2.1	1.5	−2.0
Latin America and the Caribbean								
Bolivia	5.9	5.1	6.2	6.4	5.3	4.2	2.8	−3.4
Brazil[b]	5.9	3.7	6.7	5.2	3.4	2.8	2.2	−4.5
Colombia	5.8	3.3	5.6	4.5	3.6	2.5	1.8	−3.8
Dominican Republic	6.8	3.8	5.8	5.0	4.4	3.5	2.6	−3.2
Ecuador	7.1	4.3	6.4	6.3	4.7	3.5	2.6	−3.8
El Salvador	4.8	4.4	6.0	5.2	3.9	3.5	2.5	−3.5
Guatemala[b]	3.1	5.6	6.9	5.6	4.2	2.8	2.7	−4.2
Mexico	6.2	4.1	6.4	6.3	4.0	2.7	2.4	−4.0
Peru	6.2	4.5	7.4	6.1	4.6	3.7	2.5	−4.9
Trinidad and Tobago	8.7	3.1	(2.3)	4.3	3.6	3.8	2.9	−0.6

Notes: Total fertility rates based on the five-year period prior to the survey. Calculations exclude events and exposure in the interview month. Numbers within parentheses were based on fewer than 100 cases.
a. Sample of women who had ever been married; estimates for all women are calculated applying the education inflation.
b. Based on women aged fifteen to forty-four.
Source: United Nations forthcoming.

been identified as a serious obstacle to fertility decline in Sub-Saharan African countries where the demand for children is still high (van de Walle and Foster 1990). A review of government policies in four domains affecting fertility in that region (girls' schooling, child health, laws affecting women's status and childbearing, and family planning) reports that fertility declines have been most rapid in the countries that have adopted multisectoral approaches in population and balanced family planning with investments in girls' education, child health, and improvements in women's status, property rights, and so forth (Scribner 1994). The study urges governments that have not yet broadened their population policies to do so because failure to act will ultimately constrain prospects for significant fertility decline and slow the transition to

Table 4-2. Women's Average Age at Marriage, Duration of Breast-feeding, and Use of Contraception, by Region and Education, in World Fertility Survey Countries, around 1980

Region and years of school completed	Age at marriage (years)	Duration of breast-feeding (months)	Contraceptive use (percent)
Africa[a]			
0	17.8	19.9	7
1–3	19.2	18.5	14
4–6	20.3	15.7	17
7 or more	23.0	13.4	27
Difference (between 7+ and 0)	5.2	−6.5	20
Latin America and the Caribbean			
0	19.5	15.0	24
1–3	19.5	12.1	33
4–6	20.4	9.1	43
7 or more	22.6	5.4	53
Difference (between 7+ and 0)	3.1	−9.6	29
Asia and Oceania			
0	20.2	20.1	16
1–3	19.5	18.4	26
4–6	20.6	16.0	28
7 or more	23.8	10.6	39
Difference (between 7+ and 0)	3.6	−9.5	23

a. Eight to twelve countries.
b. Thirteen countries.
c. Eight to twelve countries.
Source: Schultz 1994, table 2-6.

low fertility that is now a population policy objective in most countries of the region.

Further analysis of the relationship between education and fertility suggests that it is more complex than the association revealed by these cross-tabulations of fertility rates by educational attainment. In her recent review of findings from research on linkages between education and fertility in developing countries, Jejeebhoy (1992) found that the net fertility impact is negative but works through a variety of channels. The impact on fertility is greatest when education offers women more than a limited role in family decisions and access to resources. Jejeebhoy also raises policy concerns about relying on changes in the distribution of educational attainment to reduce fertility even though some fertility decline can be expected because of such changes. Although the proportion of poorly educated women in the developing world is declining, these women still comprise the majority in many countries, and further declines in fertility depend on their attitudes and behaviors.

Changing Reproductive Attitudes and Behaviors

In the analysis of fertility determinants, an important development in the interpretation of these data is the recognition that the effects of public policy interventions on fertility are mediated by a set of intermediate or proximate determinants of fertility, as elaborated by John Bongaarts (1978). This perspective has shifted the focus of research on fertility determinants from direct to indirect linkages, taking account of certain physiological and demographic factors through which the direct determinants affect reproductive outcomes. These are (a) use of contraceptive methods, (b) intended or involuntary infertility and interruption of pregnancy, and (c) patterns of marriage and cohabitation. Both socioeconomic conditions and programs affect these proximate variables, and Bongaarts, Mauldin, and Phillips (1990) have tried to focus the discussion of policy options on these channels and their interactions in order to inform decisions about policy and resource allocation.

In the early 1960s, fewer than 10 percent of married women in the reproductive age groups in developing countries practiced any form of fertility regulation (modern or traditional methods). By 1990, the figure was in excess of 50 percent, or just below 40 percent if China is not included. The most recent estimate of contraceptive prevalence in developing countries is 55 percent. These averages mask further shifts from traditional to modern methods and, in some instances, the more effective use of traditional methods. Other factors, including changes in marriage patterns, breast-feeding and postpartum abstinence, and the practice of abortion also account for some of the fertility decline. Overall, their impact is smaller than that of the increase in fertility regulation, although the relative impact of each on fertility levels varies at different stages of the fertility transition.

There are cases (for example, in several Latin American countries) in which the initial impact of increased use of contraceptives on fertility was dampened by offsetting declines in two fertility-limiting practices: prolonged breast-feeding and postpartum abstinence. Social and economic changes that motivate use of contraceptives—urbanization, structural changes in production, increased female education and labor force participation, and increased access to modern media—also contribute to declines in these traditional practices, which provide a natural contraceptive effect. In Sub-Saharan Africa, fertility has risen as a result of declines in these practices and in subfecundity associated with reproductive tract infections (Dyson and Murphy 1985).

Abortion is also a factor in fertility regulation, although its impact on fertility decline is difficult to assess because it is often illegal or performed clandestinely and is generally underreported in survey data. Many family planning programs seek to provide safe, effective contraception as a measure to reduce abortion. At the same time, the poor quality of services and lack of appropriate methods and counseling have led to high rates of contraceptive failure and to women resorting to abortion of unwanted pregnancies. In Latin America, where this problem is widespread, it is estimated that as much as one-quarter of recent fertility decline has resulted from increased reliance on abortion. Abortion is also significant in China, India, and Viet Nam.

Large regional differences are also evident in the average age at marriage, with later marriage more common in East Asia and Latin America and earlier marriage more common in South Asia and Sub-Saharan Africa. Differences in the average age at marriage reflect both cultural and socioeconomic factors. Socioeconomic changes that are particularly important to raising the age at marriage include increased education and employment opportunities for women and urbanization. Later marriage is found among more-educated groups in most countries. Although increases in age at marriage have generally played a lesser role in initiating recent fertility declines in developing countries than they did historically in many more developed regions, important exceptions include several East Asian and Maghrebi countries. There is also evidence that later age at marriage and first birth has contributed to incipient fertility declines in some Sub-Saharan African countries (Westoff 1992).

Underlying these changes in the proximate determinants of fertility are broad shifts in attitudes and aspirations. Most of the evidence on fertility aspirations is for married women. Survey data indicate that desired family size has been falling everywhere over the last ten to fifteen years (see table 4-3). Desired family size is highest in Sub-Saharan Africa, although even there the average for several countries fell from 7.6 children to 5.8 between the

late-1970s/early-1980s and the late-1980s/early-1990s. In some cases, the decline was quite dramatic; in Kenya, for example, desired family size dropped
from 7.2 in 1977 to 4.4 in 1989. Reflecting the low level of contraceptive use,
the fall in desired fertility in this region exceeded the fall in actual fertility
(from 7.0 to 6.7). In Asia, the decline in desired family size was from 3.9 children to 3.8, but here, because the starting point was lower and programs better
established, the decline in actual fertility was faster than that of desired fertility (from 5.4 to 4.1), bringing actual and desired fertility to nearly the same
point by the early 1990s. In Latin America and the Caribbean, the decline in
desired family size was 32 percent, from 4.3 to 3.0 children. In the Middle
East and North Africa, the decline was slightly less, from 4.5 to 3.3 children,
or 27 percent. Although declines have occurred both among the youngest (fifteen to nineteen years) and oldest (forty-five to forty-nine years) women, declines among the youngest age groups have been such that in several countries
desired fertility is approaching replacement level. This is the case in Bangladesh and Colombia (given as examples in table 4-2) and in Indonesia, Korea, Mexico, and Sri Lanka (included in the averages). In Turkey, desired
family size is already below replacement for the youngest age group.

   Another indicator of the motivation to regulate fertility can be derived
from questions on whether and when a woman wants to have another child
(table 4-3, column 4). During the 1970s, the proportion of women who said
they wanted no more children was low in the Sub-Saharan African countries
where data existed: none had more than 20 percent in that category. In Latin
America, the proportion was higher, above 45 percent for all countries except
Paraguay. In Asia, the pattern was mixed, reflecting mortality conditions.
Where infant mortality was higher and represented an obstacle to the attainment of reproductive aspirations, the proportion wanting no more children
ranged from 30 to 40 percent (for example, in Indonesia). In countries where
mortality was lower, the proportions were higher: 77 percent in Korea and 61
percent in Sri Lanka and Thailand. Bangladesh shows both higher infant mortality and a higher proportion of women wanting no more children, perhaps a
reflection of the more severe economic constraints on family size and possibly
also the result of messages conveyed through the country's vigorous family
planning program.

   In all regions of the world, the proportions wanting no more children had
risen by the late 1980s. For countries included in table 4-3, the increase was
greatest in Latin America (from 51 to 60 percent) and in Sub-Saharan Africa
(from 16 to 25 percent). Latin America currently has the world's highest proportion of women wanting no more children, and Sub-Saharan Africa has the
lowest. Gains were more modest elsewhere: from 54 to 57 percent in Asia and
45 to 50 percent in the Middle East and North Africa. In Latin America, seven

Table 4-3. Desired Number of Children and Total Fertility Rates, by Region, Late 1970s and 1980s

Region	Desired number of children			Women who want no more children (percent)	Total fertility rate
	Women 15–19	Women 45–49	All women		
Africa					
Late 1970s	6.9	8.1	7.6	15.6	7.0
Late 1980s	5.2	7.0	5.8	24.5	6.7
Ghana					
1978	5.2	7.3	6.0	12.0	6.5
1988	4.7	6.5	5.3	19.0	6.4
Kenya					
1977	6.6	8.7	7.2	18.0	8.1
1989	3.7	5.3	4.4	46.0	7.0
Asia					
Late 1970s	3.3	4.6	3.9	54.0	5.4
Late 1980s	2.8	4.1	3.8	57.0	4.1
Bangladesh					
1975	3.7	5.0	4.1	62.0	6.9
1989	2.5	3.5	2.9	55.0	5.3
Indonesia					
1976	3.3	5.0	4.2	39.0	4.8
1991	2.5	3.7	3.1	54.0	3.3
Latin America and the Caribbean					
Late 1970s	3.3	5.6	4.3	51.0	5.2
Late 1980s	2.5	3.8	3.0	60.0	3.9
Colombia					
1976	2.7	5.7	4.0	61.0	4.2
1991	2.2	3.5	2.6	64.0	3.0
Mexico					
1976	3.8	5.8	4.4	56.0	6.2
1987	2.6	4.0	3.0	65.0	3.6
Middle East and North Africa					
Late 1970s	3.9	5.3	4.5	45.0	5.7
Late 1980s	3.1	3.9	3.3	50.0	4.6
Egypt					
1980	3.6	4.8	4.1	54.0	5.2
1988	3.0	3.3	2.9	61.0	4.5
Tunisia					
1978	3.7	4.4	4.1	37.0	5.7
1988	3.1	4.0	3.5	42.0	4.0

Note: Regional averages are unweighted. Africa includes Cameroon, Ghana, Kenya, Nigeria, and Senegal; Asia includes Bangladesh, Indonesia, Nepal, Pakistan, Republic of Korea, Sri Lanka, and Thailand; Latin America and the Caribbean includes Bolivia, Colombia, the Dominican Republic, Ecuador, Jamaica, Mexico, Paraguay, and Peru; Middle East and North Africa includes Egypt, Jordan, Morocco, Tunisia, and Turkey.
Source: Calculations from various World Fertility Surveys and Demographic and Health Surveys.

countries saw increases ranging from 9 to 17 percentage points. In other regions, fewer countries registered such gains. Among those that did were Indonesia, where the increase was 15 percentage points, and Egypt, where it was 7. The most dramatic increase of all was in Kenya, with a 28 percentage point gain, from 18 percent who said they wanted no more children to 46 percent.

Survey data also show that although women may state a preference for limiting or spacing births, by no means do all practice fertility regulation. Demographers have applied the label "unmet need" to this gap between stated preferences and actual practice. Definitions vary, but most refer to the proportion of respondents who are considered to be at risk of becoming pregnant, because they state that they wish to limit or space their births but are not using any method (modern or traditional) at the time. Included in the measure are currently pregnant and breast-feeding women who state that their pregnancy was unplanned or unwanted. Although these women are not currently at risk of becoming pregnant, they are, in fact, among the most likely to resort to abortion or to have another unplanned or unwanted pregnancy if they do not adopt a contraceptive method.

As shown in table 4-4, estimates of the gap vary considerably among regions. With the exception of Sub-Saharan Africa, where it began low and has remained so (8 percent), the gap related to limiting births has been declining in all regions (most recently averaging around 11 percent). The declines have been greater in Asia, where the gap fell by half, and in Latin America, where the decline was about 30 percent. This suggests that a higher proportion of the family planning needs of limiters was being supplied or that the proportion of spacers in the reproductive-age population increased during the interval. Again with the exception of Sub-Saharan Africa, the gap for spacing is slightly lower than that for limiting (averaging 9 percent in recent years). By contrast, unmet need for spacing in Sub-Saharan Africa is at about 20 percent of at-risk women. The total (limiting and spacing combined) is about 20 percent in regions other than Sub-Saharan Africa and 28 percent there.

Caution is required in interpreting this information. Some have interpreted the combined numbers of women with an unmet need and those actually using a method as a measure of the demand, or potential demand, for services. Economists object to use of the terms "demand" and "need" in these measurements because of the absence of any information on the price of achieving their stated preferences. Respondents say they want to limit fertility, but that entails costs, both financial and psychological. Family planning programs can raise contraceptive use by lowering these costs. But the surveys from which measurements of desired family size are gleaned do not collect information on the motivation of respondents to follow through on these stated preferences. In order to understand the demand for contraception, one

Table 4-4. Sexually Active Women Not Using Contraception, by Fertility Preferences, 1980 and 1990

(percentage)

Region	Limiters[a] 1980	1990	Spacers,[b] 1990	Limiters and spacers, 1990
Africa	8.0	8.0	20.0	28.0
Asia	19.0	9.0	9.0	18.0
Latin America and the Caribbean	18.0	13.0	8.0	21.0
Middle East and North Africa	15.0	12.0	10.0	22.0

a. Women who want no more children.
b. Women who want to delay next birth for two or more years.
Source: For 1980 data, World Fertility Surveys for nine countries in Sub-Saharan Africa, ten countries in Asia, thirteen countries in Latin America and the Caribbean, and six countries in the Middle East and North Africa. For 1990 data, Demographic and Health Surveys for eleven countries in Sub-Saharan Africa, four countries in the Middle East and North Africa.

needs to know how much it would be worth to these women to prevent a birth. Without such information, one has no sense of what prices respondents are using in these hypothetical answers and what the probable response would be to lowering the costs of fertility regulation.

For example, in cases where the net costs of children are low, even though a woman states in a survey interview (most interviewees are women) that she would like no more children, her motivation or willingness to prevent additional births may also be low. It could turn out to be very costly for programs to lower the cost of fertility regulation sufficiently to induce such women to act on stated desires. However, another woman for whom the net costs of children are already very high might be very motivated (and willing to pay) to prevent a birth. Even a small reduction in the cost of fertility regulation might be sufficient for her to act on her stated intentions. Even more fundamentally, the reasons why these women or men are not using contraception may have little to do with costs that programs can easily address.

Thus, conventional measures of this gap or unmet need may substantially overstate the potential demand response of women to policies that lower the costs of fertility regulation. They also fail to consider the potential responses of women who do not state a willingness to limit or space births, but who nevertheless might respond to a change in the costs of fertility regulation. By focusing on women who state that they want no more children, program managers may be neglecting the potential response of women who have not stated such a preference but who might be easily influenced to practice fertility regulation.

Research on the reasons why survey respondents are not using a method in spite of their stated intention to space or limit births is scarce but is attracting increased attention. To the extent that information on the gap between aspirations and practices points to deficiencies on the supply side, it can help program managers to determine why respondents are not using contraceptives and to devise ways of removing those obstacles. In the survey data cited above, the majority of respondents who have used a temporary method but discontinued it cite fear of side effects, partners' disapproval, inconvenience, and other concerns, including the moral acceptability of available methods. This should signal program managers that they need to provide a broader range of methods or to improve the counseling on existing methods if the problem is inaccurate information. Access to services and costs of methods were also cited but were generally less important. Among women who have never used a method, however, the proportion citing lack of access and high cost was higher. These findings are consistent with recent analyses of service availability data collected for a number of countries in the second round of Demographic and Health Surveys. They indicate that the type of facility and the kinds of services offered are more important determinants than their existence or location. They also indicate that the quality of services may be a more important determinant of use or nonuse than the distance or travel time between client residences and the point of service delivery, a finding that is confirmed in a growing body of operations research on the quality of services in a number of countries (Wilkinson and others 1993).

Women's health advocates have recommended that programs target all nonusers of contraception who are at risk of an unplanned pregnancy (see Dixon-Mueller and Germain 1992). An estimated 20 percent of unmarried women in reproductive ages, most of them adolescents, who are not included in standard measures of the gap between aspirations and practice, are estimated to be at risk of an unwanted pregnancy. Another group to which they call attention is women who report that they use a reversible method but are not using the method effectively or are likely to stop using it because of dissatisfaction with the method, a partner's disapproval, fear of side effects, difficulties in getting supplies of the method, or method failure. Discontinuation of methods and method failure due to improper use are factors in the high incidence of unsafe abortions in developing countries. As noted earlier in this chapter, an estimated 20 percent of pregnancies in developing countries end in abortion, and close to half of these are performed under unsafe conditions (see Sundström 1993).

An analysis of Demographic and Health Survey data sponsored by the International Planned Parenthood Federation for twelve countries suggests that more than half the users of reversible methods were likely to stop using the method within a year. The findings indicate that as many as 111 million of the 200 million users of such methods in developing countries fall into this category. The report attributes the problem mainly to the poor quality of family planning services: too little counseling, limited choice of method, and poor follow-up for clients relying on methods that must be resupplied (IPPF 1993).

Evidence from Country-Level Studies

Cross-national comparisons provide at best indicative evidence of the interplay between supply and demand factors in promoting fertility decline; they do not tell us much about how the two sets of forces may have interacted with each other during the two decades over which recent fertility declines occurred. This has generated renewed interest in understanding the interplay of supply and demand factors at both the community and household levels, and particularly in how those interactions may have changed over time.

For example, a recent Bank-supported study on Indonesia (Gertler and Molyneaux 1994) concluded that increased education and women's earnings opportunities contributed much more than family planning expenditures to that country's fertility decline during the mid-1980s. They noted, however, that the impact of education came about in the context of an already well-developed program of family planning services. A similar story emerges from the experience of Kenya, whose early investments in both education and family planning are paying off in the more rapid decline of fertility during the last decade (see Kelley and Nobbe 1990). Studies have also noted that family planning subsidies contribute to narrowing of fertility differentials between more- and less-educated groups in countries that have experienced general declines in fertility (see Schultz 1992).

What the experiences of countries where fertility has declined rapidly over the last two decades reveal is that both supply and demand influences are at work, that they are mutually reinforcing, and that their relative importance varies according to the country's social and economic conditions, including where it is in the fertility transition process (see Cleland 1993; Simmons 1992). To learn from such experiences, social policy needs to be informed about linkages between use of fertility regulation and the larger social context in which reproductive choices are made. This understanding would be considerably easier if the fertility transition and broader social changes that affect it took place in an even, orderly fashion across all groups in a society. Unfortunately, that does not usually happen. Some groups lead, others follow. The

Figure 4-1.   Contraceptive Prevalence in Bangladesh, by Level of Education, 1982–91

Percent

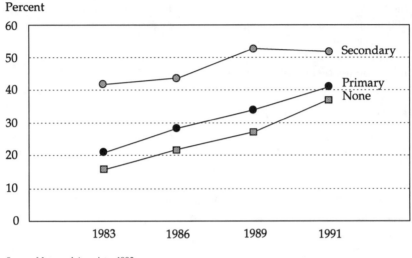

Source: Matra and Associates 1992.

benefits of expanded access to *both* education and family planning typically accrue to groups who are in a relatively privileged position: the sons and daughters of the educated are more likely to be in school.

Low female education and women's status are major constraints to fertility decline in many African and South Asian countries where the demand for children is high and the demand for fertility regulation is still limited. Over the long run, investments in education and other improvements in women's status will be needed to stimulate demand for smaller families. At the same time, the experience of Bangladesh (see figure 4-1; box 4-1) has demonstrated that a vigorous family planning program can increase contraceptive prevalence despite an adverse demand setting.

The relevant question for policy is how supply of contraceptives and demand for children interact in different settings. Where demand is preexisting, the introduction of services by the public sector or other changes such as the removal of legal restrictions on the provision of services by the private sector may lead to a rapid adoption of fertility regulation. Where demand is limited to a small segment of society, motivational efforts will be required.

As noted, the interplay of supply and demand factors does not remain

---

BOX 4-1. SUCCESS IN A CHALLENGING
ENVIRONMENT: FERTILITY DECLINE IN
BANGLADESH

In the 1970s, many experts doubted that the transition to low fertility could occur soon in Bangladesh, which was one of the world's poorest countries, with a total fertility rate of seven.

During the 1980s, Bangladesh demonstrated that with sustained political commitment and a creative approach, fertility decline could be accelerated. Its program reaches out to village women (employing local women as outreach workers) with family planning and other services that respond to reproductive health needs. Although involving higher costs during its experimental stage, the approach is being replicated throughout Bangladesh and incorporates a number of interventions in addition to family planning services.

Figure 4-1 shows how this strategy has succeeded even with an unfavorable social setting. While demonstrating the high correlation between fertility regulation and educational level, it also shows that outreach to less-educated women can narrow the educational gap. This is important for Bangladesh, because individuals whose behavior will determine fertility over the next decade are already in their reproductive ages.

At the same time, it is unlikely that Bangladesh can complete its transition to low fertility without increased female education and other improvements in women's status. Policymakers are now seeking ways to balance these needs with the need to improve and expand reproductive health services (see Cleland and others 1994).

---

static. The timing of policies is also important, because policies such as education and those that affect the role and status of women have a long gestation period and need to be started early. This may also be true of the institutional infrastructure needed to expand service availability to large segments of the population. Countries in East and Southeast Asia and in Latin America that were investing in both education and family planning during the 1960s and 1970s saw the most dramatic declines in fertility during the 1980s. The incipient fertility declines in Sub-Saharan Africa have occurred in countries such as Kenya and Zimbabwe that were investing in both education and family planning. While improved access and quality in family planning and reproductive health services will help to stimulate the practice of fertility regulation and bring important health and welfare benefits to African families, it is unlikely that the region will complete the transition to low fertility unless these efforts are balanced by investments in education and other social sectors.

The answer to the question about the relative importance of supply and demand factors in fertility decline is not "either/or" but rather "both" and, even better, a balance of both that is responsive to the specific needs and conditions of different countries at different levels of the demographic transition and socioeconomic development. Country-specific strategies are required to address these needs as countries move from high to low fertility, and this requires a continuing effort to reassess the mix of policies and programs at the country level.

CHAPTER FIVE

Social Policy
and Population

$\mathbf{P}$OVERTY reduction and sustained economic growth are important prerequisites for human development and have a strong influence on
population growth prospects. Motivation to have smaller families is linked to
perceptions that the family will be better off with fewer but better-nourished
and better-educated children. If those expectations are frustrated by poverty,
the messages in motivational campaigns promoting smaller families quickly
become discredited. Also, because of the very large numbers being added to
the populations of poor countries, improvements in living standards will be
impossible without sustained economic growth and broad efforts to reduce
poverty.

This view is supported by the experience that attended recent declines in
fertility in East and Southeast Asia and in many Latin American countries
during the 1970s and 1980s. These declines were accompanied by rapid economic and social changes. Fertility declines were most rapid in countries
where there was a supportive social policy environment; improvements in the
status of women through increased education, access to credit and earnings
opportunities, and breaking down of legal and cultural barriers to women's
participation in the development process illustrate the kinds of supportive
changes that are needed.

These findings are also consistent with the conclusions of the World
Bank's review of its own experience in population work (World Bank 1992b).
Based on case studies of countries for which the Bank has provided loans for
investments in population (Bangladesh, India, Indonesia, and Kenya) and sev-

67

eral others in which the Bank has played a lesser role (Brazil, Colombia, Mexico, and Senegal), this work concluded that although supply-oriented strategies may have been sufficient to build on the latent demand for fertility regulation at early stages of fertility transitions, more emphasis on the demand side would be necessary to complete those transitions. In particular, it urged the Bank to pay greater attention to selective interventions in the development process that could change the implicit benefits and costs of large families, noting that the Bank is uniquely qualified to pursue these broader approaches.

Further, the report reinforced the message of several other country studies about the timing of investments in family planning, reproductive health, and education as they affect reproductive behavior. Although the transition to lower fertility is occurring much more rapidly in developing countries than it did in countries whose transitions occurred before World War II, those developing countries that succeeded in complementing their early efforts in family planning with parallel investments in supportive social sectors like education and health have experienced the most rapid fertility declines. Even if the full impact of demand-side interventions are not felt until the middle stages of the transition process, the lag between the time when girls are in school and the time when schooling affects their reproductive behavior requires that those investments be made well in advance of the time when fertility declines slow down once the initial pool of demand has been met by supply-side interventions.

A supportive socioeconomic environment is likewise important for successful program efforts. A series of cross-national studies carried out by Parker Mauldin in collaboration with his colleagues Bernard Berelson, Robert Lapham, and John Ross demonstrates the complementarities between broader socioeconomic forces and program-related variables in the rapid fertility declines that have occurred over the last two decades. These studies examine the effects on fertility of standard measures of progress in socioeconomic development (including literacy, school enrollment ratios, infant mortality, life expectancy, urbanization, nonagricultural employment, and gross national product per capita) in conjunction with program-effort indicators, which measure access to and quality of services and information as well as other characteristics of programs (see Mauldin and Ross 1991).

Table 5-1 presents the most recent compilation of the Mauldin-Ross measures. In that table, countries are classified by the level of program effort and the strength of the social setting; the percentage decline in the total fertility rate between 1975 and 1990 is shown for each country listed. Although a great deal of care is needed in drawing conclusions from aggregate cross-national measures, it is clear that the countries with the most rapid fertility declines cluster in the upper left-hand segment of the table where the indicators for social setting and program effort are both high and that countries in the lower right-hand segment, where those indicators are low, have had very little fertility decline. The table also suggests that some countries with less favorable socioeconomic conditions have experienced fertility declines when program effort was stronger, while others have done so with lower program effort but a strong social setting.

Analysis of the data presented in the table has also confirmed that there is a high correlation between social setting and program effort. This supports the view that social and economic conditions affect not only the demand but also the supply side of the fertility and family planning equations. Stronger programs are found where underlying conditions are supportive. Higher levels of education, for example, contribute to improving management capacity and to increasing the pool of qualified service-delivery personnel (see Subbarao and Raney 1993).

Poverty Reduction and Human Development Strategies

Much of the ambiguity described earlier in this report about the extent to which population growth affects poverty stems from the complexity and circularity of the causal links. High rates of population growth are associated with poverty, and high fertility is a characteristic of poor households. Poverty reduction strategies, in fact, focus on many of the same investments in human resource development that are needed for the broader approach to population policy outlined above. The World Bank's *World Development Report 1990: Poverty* and its follow-up documents, *Assistance Strategies to Reduce Poverty* and *The Poverty Reduction Handbook*, articulate a two-pronged strategy for sustainable poverty reduction (World Bank, 1991, 1993c). First, broadly based economic growth is required to generate efficient income-earnings opportunities for the poor. Second, improved access to education, health care, and other social services helps the poor take advantage of these opportunities. Both elements are designed to develop and use effectively the poor's most abundant asset: their labor. The strategy also calls for creation of social safety nets for the most vulnerable groups.

Bank experience in poverty reduction points to a number of important operational lessons, beginning with the need for analyses of policies, public expenditures, and institutional capacity from a poverty-reduction perspective. Particular attention needs to be given to the efficiency of incentives and the cost-effectiveness of public expenditures. Analytical work is also required to identify programs and projects that benefit the poor and do not divert resources intended for poverty reduction to other groups. For this reason, monitoring and evaluation are important for successful implementation of such ac-

Table 5-1. Percentage Decline in Total Fertility Rate among Developing Countries in 1975–90, by Social Setting in 1985 and Level of Program Effort in 1989

Social setting	Strong		Moderate		Weak		Very weak or none	
	Country	Decline	Country	Decline	Country	Decline	Country	Decline
High	Korea, Rep. of	51	Korea, Dem. People's Rep. of	46	Brazil	26	Kuwait	43
	Taiwan	43	Jamaica	44	Jordan	23	Iraq	13
	Mexico	41	Cuba	34				
	Mauritius	38	Panama	33				
			Colombia	31				
			Costa Rica	24				
			Venezuela	23				
			Lebanon	22				
			Singapore	20				
			Chile	18				
			Trinidad and Tobago	15				
Mean decline		43		28		24		28
Upper middle	Thailand	48	Guyana	42	Algeria	29	Libya	10
	China	38	Peru	33	Turkey	27	Saudi Arabia	2
	Tunisia	37	Dominican Republic	31	Paraguay	17		
	Sri Lanka	34	Ecuador	29	Syrian Arab Republic	14		
	Indonesia	33	Egypt	21	Congo	0		
	Botswana	28	Iran	21				
	El Salvador	21	Philippines	20				
			Malaysia	19				
			Zimbabwe	19				
			Guatemala	13				
Mean decline		34		26		17		6

India	18	Honduras	25	Haiti	12	Cambodia	5
		Kenya	17	Bolivia	8	Liberia	1
		Pakistan	11	Nigeria	2	Côte d'Ivoire	0
		Ghana	3	Madagascar	1	Laos	−4
		Zambia	−2	Zaire	0		
				Lesotho	−1		
				Tanzania	−1		
				Cameroon	−6		
				Central African Republic	−7		
Mean decline	25		14		2		6
Low							
Bangladesh	22	Nepal	12	Senegal	10	Sudan	5
				Afghanistan	5	Chad	2
				Mozambique	3	Somalia	0
				Rwanda	3	Malawi	−1
				Benin	0		
				Burkina Faso	2		
				Ethiopia	2		
				Burundi	0		
				Guinea	0		
				Mali	0		
				Mauritania	0		
				Niger	0		
				Sierra Leone	0		
				Togo	0		
				Uganda	−3		
				Guinea-Bissau	−6		
Mean decline	22		12		1		1
Mean	34		24		5		8

Note: Means were calculated by unit weights. Negative entries indicate a rise in the total fertility rate.
Source: Mauldin and Ross 1991.

tivities. Also central is involvement of client groups from among the poor and coordination with other agencies involved in poverty reduction.

Investments in human development are central to the Bank's poverty reduction strategy. In addition to the integrated approach to reproductive health outlined in the next chapter, three policy objectives that are particularly important in relation to population are (1) to eliminate the gender gap in education, (2) to empower women, reduce gender disparities, and enhance women's participation in the benefits of economic development, and (3) to reduce infant and child mortality.

Eliminating the Gender Gap in Education

The pivotal role of education as a determinant of reproductive attitudes and practice has already been addressed, as have the major obstacles that stand in the way of fertility reduction because of low levels of female literacy and educational attainment. In addition to the direct effects discussed earlier, these limitations also affect fertility indirectly through a variety of channels, for example, their adverse effects on the earnings and income-generation capacities of poor households. These barriers are particularly serious in the poorest countries of Sub-Saharan Africa and in poorer parts of South Asia, the Middle East, and Latin America.

Evidence on the extent of the gender gap in education is provided by King and Hill (1993) in their study of women's education in developing countries. Table 5-2 shows that the gap is greatest in low-income countries with low levels of educational attainment. Both low income and low levels of education are inversely associated with fertility decline, although there are clearly exceptions that reflect other factors such as culture and the availability of family planning services. Bangladesh stands out among low-income countries because of its combination of high fertility decline and large gender gap in education. In fact, that gap has raised concerns about the likelihood of Bangladesh's finishing the transition to low fertility and has motivated efforts described earlier in this report to broaden the focus of that country's population policy. This concern has also been voiced about other countries that have experienced some success in reducing fertility but that maintain large gender gaps (Algeria, Iraq, Morocco, and Tunisia), although the effect of the gender gap is offset to some extent by the higher general level of education in those countries. Clearly efforts are required on both fronts, and the goal of attaining universal primary education for all addresses both issues.

Several World Bank reports suggest strategies for achieving these objectives. For example, the report *Letting Girls Learn* provides a strong case for investing in girls' education as a means of lowering fertility rates as well as

construction of new schools and training of additional teachers as well as to address specific constraints that keep girls out of school. Local conditions will determine the specific investments needed, but the combined goals of providing universal primary education and bridging the gender gap in education are achievable development objectives with enormous societal and individual benefits. A study prepared for the World Conference on Education for All held in Jomtien, Thailand, in 1990 estimates that the additional aid required to achieve universal primary education would amount to around $30 billion during the period 1990–2005, of which about half would go to Africa. The calculations imply aid flows of about $2.5 billion a year over that fifteen-year interval and assume that developing countries receiving this aid would match it with their own investments as well as introduce complementary packages of cost-saving and cost-shifting reforms (Colclough 1993). Much of the needed financing could be mobilized by redirecting allocations from public subsidies to activities inside and outside education that the private sector could deliver more effectively. During the 1990s, there has been a major shift in donor assistance from the secondary and tertiary levels of education to the primary level. During the 1980s, more than 85 percent of donor assistance was directed to the former, while primary education remained generally neglected.

Empowering Women

Full realization of the benefits of increased female educational attainment for women's productive and reproductive roles in society requires the removal of obstacles that deprive women of the benefits of economic development and inhibit their capacity to be effective partners with their husbands in household decisionmaking and resource allocation. Analyses of the ways in which education influences reproductive behavior emphasize the importance of improvements in the status of women as a condition for education to have its expected effects. It also requires empowerment of women through better legal protection for young girls and unmarried women, improvements in reproductive health and counseling services, commitment by parents and community leaders, and, most important, changes in the attitudes and practices of men.

Inequality at both the household and community levels has direct and indirect effects on reproductive behavior. Although education contributes to increased autonomy for women and increases their chances to exercise greater control over their reproductive decisions, the effects of increased education can be muted by legal, regulatory, and cultural obstacles to women's full participation in civil society. Removal of such obstacles has been shown to have a positive reinforcing effect on national fertility declines, as in the case of Tunisia, where strong social legislation and complementary investments in female education, child health, and family planning contributed to a 33 percent decline in the total fertility rate between 1978 and 1988 (see box 5-2; Cochrane and Guilkey 1992).

The Bank's policy paper on gender issues, *Participation in Enhancing Women's Economic Development*, provides additional information on measures to improve women's status and participation in economic activity (World Bank 1994b). That paper calls on governments and donors to develop gender-sensitive policies and programs. These policies need to go beyond gender-neutral investments in health and education to address disparities that directly and indirectly affect women. It also calls for measures to eliminate legal and regulatory barriers to women's full participation in the labor market, to enable rural women to gain title to the land they farm, and to make it possible for women to obtain credit and other financial assistance for income-generating and consumption activities.

Better information and analysis of gender issues are needed to design and evaluate program and policy changes and to mobilize the resources required to implement them. The report also notes the important role that women have played in service delivery in the social sectors, including health, family planning, and education, and urges more effort to expand training and deployment of female providers. Nongovernmental organizations, many of them run by women, have a critical role to play in this effort, and the report urges the Bank and borrowers to seek greater collaboration with them in these areas.

Reducing Infant and Child Mortality

High infant and child mortality rates are another well-recognized factor in the persistence of high fertility in poor countries. When child death rates are high

---

BOX 5-2. EXAMPLES OF SUPPORTIVE LEGISLATIVE CHANGES IN TUNISIA

Personal Status Code (1956): Granted women civil status of majority, abrogated polygamy and abandonment, established legal divorce, forbade marriage of preadolescent girls, granted freedom of choice of spouse.

Education Law (1958): Established a plan to increase school attendance, though without mandatory attendance requirements.

Contraceptive Law (1961): Legalized the importation, sale, and distribution of contraceptives.

Marriage Law (1964): Raised minimum age of marriage to seventeen for women and twenty for men.

Source: Cochrane and Guilkey 1992.

and child survival uncertain, parents tend to be fatalistic about reproductive decisions and compensate for the possibility of losing children by having more of them. When mortality rates are falling, couples tend to overcompensate. They are also less likely to invest in their children's health and education. Investment to increase child survival contributes to lower fertility at the individual level, if measures to improve child survival are combined with family planning information to help mothers adjust their reproductive aspirations as a higher proportion of their children survive. No country has completed the transition to low fertility without parallel declines in infant and child mortality rates, although the causal linkages between the two are mutually reinforcing. Child spacing and avoidance of high-risk births contribute to increased child survival.

Where family planning and other maternal/child health services are integrated, they can build on these mutually reinforcing relationships between lower fertility and improved child health, in particular by encouraging practices with multiple benefits for both mother and child (see box 5-3). Breastfeeding is an example in that it both improves nutrition and has traditionally been used to space births. In so doing, it has had a powerful reducing effect on fertility at the national level. Other maternal and child health interventions, such as nutrition supplements, immunization, and oral rehydration therapy, also play similar mutually reinforcing roles. These interventions are highly cost-effective, as shown in *World Development Report 1993*, and offer a range

---

BOX 5-3. MUTUALLY REINFORCING INTERVENTIONS: NUTRITION IN TAMIL NADU, INDIA

The state of Tamil Nadu in India recently joined two other Indian states, Kerala and Goa, that have reached replacement-level fertility. Goa, a very small state, and Kerala, with its high literacy and more equitable income distribution, have been considered exceptions to general conditions in India. When Tamil Nadu joined the low-fertility club, people began to look for other answers.

One has turned up in Tamil Nadu's well-publicized push to overcome malnutrition, which has included a school-based noontime meal program that motivated parents to send girls to school (in part because they could bring some food home for younger siblings). Not only did the program achieve its intended objective of reducing malnutrition, but analysts now believe that it also contributed to increased educational attainment of girls and, through that, to a faster transition to lower fertility among women who benefited from the program when they were girls.

of benefits in addition to their direct and indirect effects on reproductive behavior (see also Cochrane and Merrick 1994).

Overall strategies to reduce infant and child mortality take advantage of similar mutually reinforcing relationships that recognize and build on the synergies between child survival and poverty reduction, increased education, and specific health sector interventions. *World Development Report 1993* documents these relationships and calls for action to finance and implement several measures that have proved to be highly cost-effective in reducing infant and child mortality as well as the disabilities that still leave hundreds of thousands of children deaf, blind, mentally retarded, or paralyzed. These include immunizations to control such childhood diseases as measles and polio, nutrition interventions to reduce iodine and Vitamin A deficiencies, proper treatment of diarrheal disease through such interventions as oral rehydration therapy, and parallel efforts to reduce iron deficiencies among mothers and neonatal tetanus. Investments to improve the safety of water and sanitation systems are also called for.

Most of this could be accomplished by allocating a higher proportion of public sector spending on health to basic public health programs and to essential clinical services rather than continuing to subsidize less cost-effective tertiary care that could be financed through user fees and insurance plans. The World Bank (1993d) estimates that the overall cost of public health interventions, including those above, are about $12 per capita in low-income countries and $22 per capita in middle-income countries.

Mobilizing Resources for Social Policy Objectives

Precise estimates of the overall resource requirements for the broader package of social sector investments just described are problematic in the face of the widely divergent institutional and financial conditions that prevail among developing countries. Still, most agree that the goal of meeting these requirements is not out of reach. The draft Cairo Conference declaration calls for developing countries and donor agencies to allocate 20 percent of their budgets to the social sectors to achieve a broad range of social policy objectives, including universal access to family planning and reproductive health services, reductions in infant and child mortality, and universal primary education (United Nations 1994). UNICEF calls for global investments of $25 billion a year by the year 2000 to reach a similar set of goals (Grant 1994).

Mobilization of the needed resources will require increased commitment and effort from the current sources of funding, plus exploration of ways to make more efficient use of existing resources. *Donors,* both bilateral and multilateral, will need to maintain their commitment to the social sectors in the face of competing priorities and pressures. *Developing countries* will also need to give higher priority to the social sectors, both through additional budgetary allocations or redirection of government funding toward interventions, such as family planning as part of a package of essential services, and through user payments for part or all of the services provided through public or private channels. *Efficiency gains* may also be possible through more effective use of existing resources. Nongovernmental organizations and other private channels can be used better to take greater advantage of their relative strengths; resource allocations within programs can be monitored better to ensure greater technical and economic efficiency.

CHAPTER SIX

Integrated Approaches in Reproductive Health

ALTHOUGH countries vary substantially in their institutional and financial capacities to provide reproductive health and family planning services and in their position in the fertility transition, in almost every country the demand for services is expanding. Contraceptive prevalence levels in East Asia (70 percent or more of married women in reproductive ages) are comparable to those in more-industrial regions, with many Latin American countries not far behind. There is more variation across South Asia and the Middle East: Bangladesh, Egypt, India, and Morocco have rates of 40 percent or more, while Pakistan and Yemen have much lower rates. Fertility regulation is practiced least in Sub-Saharan Africa, although there are signs of change. Botswana, Kenya, and Zimbabwe experienced significant increases in contraceptive prevalence during the 1980s.

Local conditions may justify government involvement in financing and delivering these services when private markets fail to provide information and methods for underserved groups or when the public interest is served by actions to accelerate fertility declines. Two operating principles have emerged from the current debate about the appropriate role of government in population policy. They offer a promising approach to achieving the needed balance between public and private interests and are fully consistent with the basic redirection of population policy toward integrated approaches at both the service delivery and broader social policy levels called for in the introduction to this report.

First, in the design and delivery of services, reproductive health needs of women, and men, should be primary (see box 6-1). As far as possible, this should be accomplished by delivering family planning services as part of an essential package of services that would include, for example, prenatal and maternity care as well as control and prevention of reproductive tract infections. The delivery of contraceptive supplies through commercial outlets, social marketing channels, and other nonclinical outlets would be possible as long as standards of quality are maintained. The point is to provide fertility regulation as a reproductive health and not a population control measure. Demographics can serve in the mapping of needs and in the design of strategies to meet them, but they should not be the goal of service delivery.

Second, when rapid population growth hampers a country's development objectives, government action to stimulate fertility reduction should be pursued as part of a broad range of social policies outlined in the previous chapter. These policies have positive benefits in their own right and have the added benefit of increasing motivation for smaller families. When actions aimed specifically at reproductive motivation or behavior are undertaken, special attention should be given to human rights concerns. Independent monitoring of potential infringements on those rights should be carried out by agents who represent the interests of affected groups.

Where government has a social interest in making family planning available, its primary responsibility lies in ensuring access to information and services rather than itself acting in every instance as financier and provider. Where the case is strong for offering public subsidy for low-income and rural groups, and more broadly for family planning information, the government's

---

BOX 6-1. WHAT IS REPRODUCTIVE HEALTH?

Within the framework of WHO's definition of health as a state of complete physical, mental and social well-being, and not merely the absence of disease or infirmity, reproductive health addresses the reproductive processes, functions, and system at all stages of life. Reproductive health therefore implies that people are able to have a responsible, satisfying, and safe sex life and that they have the capability to reproduce and the freedom to decide if, when, and how often to do so. Implicit in this last condition are the right of men and women to be informed of and to have access to safe, effective, affordable, and acceptable methods of fertility regulation of their choice, and the right of access to appropriate health care services that will enable women to go safely through pregnancy and childbirth and provide couples with the best chance of having a healthy infant.

(World Health Organization)

role may not necessarily be to act as sole provider but to encourage the most efficient private/public sector mix. In countries whose governments play a more active role in the provision of health services, reproductive health and family planning should be included among them. Where the private sector plays a more prominent role, government involvement may still be required to provide financial support or to remove legal and regulatory obstacles to information and services, including medical regulations that unnecessarily increase the amount of time and money that individuals have to expend.

Addressing Broader Reproductive Health Needs

It is now widely accepted that family planning programs must meet a wide range of the reproductive health needs of women and men. Thus, many programs now attempt to provide counseling and support in such related areas as breast-feeding, child survival, and safe motherhood. In addition, programs increasingly have had to address other health concerns related to sexual activity and reproduction. Prominent among these concerns is the need to deal with the HIV/AIDS epidemic and with reproductive tract infections that have serious health repercussions and contribute to the risk of HIV infection.

Likewise, the scope of programs is being expanded to groups whose needs have not been served by traditional modes of service provision. Adolescents, for example, are at high risk of exposure to unwanted pregnancy and reproductive tract infections but are often inhibited from approaching providers who are oriented to the needs of married couples. Males, particularly those who engage in high-risk sexual behavior, are another poorly served group, with adolescent males being the least served of all. As the seriousness of the HIV/AIDS epidemic is grasped by policymakers and program planners—not just for high-risk-behavior males but for their wives and children as well—traditional modes of delivering family planning and reproductive health services are being modified.

As more is required of service delivery systems, the organizational challenges increase as well. For example, logistics systems must be devised, providers trained, and counseling made available. Procedures to assure the quality of services are needed. Communication campaigns to explain family planning and reproductive health practices must complement service provision. The majority of programs involve not just one organization but several, with public and private groups providing services through an increasing range of facilities, from clinics to pharmacies to individual home visitors.

Reproductive health and fertility regulation involve more than the provision of information and services. Many social factors affect contraceptive acceptance and reproductive behavior. Addressing these factors through a variety of human resource programs helps reduce the demand for children and increase the demand for fertility regulation and other services. Services such as programs to promote breast-feeding, child survival, and safe motherhood are generally the responsibility of health ministries. Where these services are integrated, they can build on the mutually reinforcing relationships between lower fertility and improved maternal and child health, in particular by encouraging practices with multiple benefits for both mother and child. Understanding the specific ways in which fertility regulation and improved reproductive health both contribute to and result from progress toward these broader goals also requires research on how they are linked in particular settings and intersectoral coordination of policies and programs.

One way that these reproductive health needs could be addressed would be as part of a comprehensive primary health care package, as recommended in *World Development Report 1993: Investing in Health* (World Bank 1993e). The report also recommends an essential package of clinical services, whose components would vary from country to country depending on local needs and level of income. Family planning and control of reproductive tract infections are included in this package. Building on this concept, a forthcoming Bank paper on best practices in women's health will recommend an essential package of women's health services that includes fertility regulation and other reproductive health services as outlined in box 6-2. Again the components of the package will vary on a country-by-country basis, depending on local needs and institutional and financial capacity (Tinker and others 1994).

BOX 6-2. ESSENTIAL WOMEN'S HEALTH PACKAGE

Services

■ Prevention/management of unwanted pregnancies, including family planning, medical termination of pregnancy (where permitted), and treatment of the complications of unsafe abortion

■ Safe pregnancy services, including prenatal care (with needed immunizations and nutrition supplementation), safe delivery, and provision for transport and referral of obstetric emergencies

■ Prevention and management of sexually transmitted diseases and reproductive tract infections, including HIV/AIDS.

Policies and public education

■ Prevention of adverse practices such as genital mutilation, violence against women, and differential care

■ Promotion of positive health practices, including child spacing, safe sex, adequate nutrition, and male involvement.

More than twenty-five years of experience in the delivery of family planning services have provided a wealth of lessons in how to meet the complex and diverse reproductive health needs of developing countries. Many of these lessons are being applied as family planning programs expand their coverage to include a broader range of reproductive health services. Effective programs have several characteristics similar to those of effective service organizations in other fields, as summarized in a recent World Bank report (World Bank 1993b).

- First, effective programs are "responsive to client needs and provide good access to [fertility regulation] methods clients want" (p. 2). Individual clients should receive not only a choice of methods but also counseling to facilitate continued use and attention to other relevant reproductive health concerns.
- Second, effective programs have an organizational structure congruent to their setting. Programs include such basic elements as a delivery system for getting contraceptives to users; a logistics network for ensuring a proper supply of commodities; a system for recruitment, training, and supervision of front-line staff; and arrangements for monitoring, evaluation, and research.
- Third, effective programs are actively and continually engaged in motivational activities. Potential beneficiaries, the public at large, and policymakers tend to be poorly informed about the benefits of fertility regulation and about such practical issues as the safety of contraceptive methods. Educating such groups about fertility regulation and other reproductive health issues requires the use of modern techniques of mass communication, together with personal contacts, to ensure that messages have a lasting impact.
- Fourth, effective public sector programs do not stand by themselves but are linked with and support parallel efforts at contraceptive distribution and promotion by nongovernmental organizations, private practitioners and facilities, and even commercial outlets for contraceptives. These private agencies provide additional service points, relieve some of the administrative and financial burden on government services, and can be a source of program innovation.

Policy Options in Emergent, Transitional, and Advanced Settings

Underlying all of these lessons is the point that there is no single ideal model of program design. Recalling the policy framework outlined in chapter 1 (table 1-1), the appropriate role for government involvement in reproductive health and family planning will depend on local circumstances and needs. Those needs shift as countries move through the different stages of the fertility transition, and policy responses should vary accordingly, as illustrated in the list of policy options outlined in the demographic setting axis of that framework:

- In emergent settings, invest in infrastructure and institutional capacity for delivering the basic package of reproductive health and family planning, pilot alternative approaches to service delivery, and develop capacity for information dissemination and public education
- In transitional settings, extend the basic package to underserved groups, increase private sector involvement, address quality issues, remove legal and regulatory obstacles, and test cost-recovery schemes.
- In advanced settings, ensure that subsidies are targeted toward underserved groups, implement sustainable financing, maintain quality, and close remaining gaps in reproductive health.

The following sections examine in more detail the changing reproductive health needs of countries at different stages of the fertility transition and discuss in more detail the responses that have been made in reproductive health as well as in broader social policy.

Emergent Settings

Countries at the initial stages of their fertility transitions are generally the poorest and have the strongest interest in speeding up the transition to lower fertility. They also face unfavorable socioeconomic and reproductive health settings, with very low levels of educational attainment and with total fertility rates typically above six, infant mortality above 100 per 1,000 live births, and maternal mortality easily twenty times the industrial-country average. Many Sub-Saharan African countries face such conditions, but they do not necessarily hold in all cases where either reproductive health or social indicators are low.

BOX 6-3. EXAMPLES OF EMERGENT SETTINGS

At the early stage of the fertility transition, borrower countries need to make basic investments in family planning and other social sectors. Some of the challenges at this stage are illustrated in Bank sector reviews for Chad, which is just entering this stage, and Kenya, which now seems to have successfully passed through it.

Chad. With political conflict still simmering, Chad has nevertheless begun to consider seriously the need for a population policy. Fertility is high but is kept down somewhat by high levels of sterility. Importing contraceptives is still illegal, a hangover from the French colonial period. Although there are no good data, public awareness of contraception appears to be more limited than perhaps anywhere else in the world. The public health system is rudimentary. At present, 80 percent of it is funded by foreign donors. Nevertheless, a blueprint for an integrated system has recently been produced (see Jarawan and others 1992).

Given continuing concerns about political stability, the Bank has approached the situation cautiously. A possible project is being developed with the Ministry of Health premised on the government's agreement to adopt a population policy and liberalize contraceptive imports. The project will have three basic thrusts: to support the development of population policy and analysis of population problems; to support private efforts to provide and promote family planning services, using a special grant fund; and to strengthen the public health system, especially through reforming pharmaceutical procurement and distribution and through providing support for health services in two particular regions, in order to complement the work of other donors. Backing up these efforts is lending in education: a component on female education, in particular, is being designed as part of a second education project.

Box 6-3, drawing on Bank sector reviews and project experience, illustrates the issues and needs in early-stage settings by contrasting a recent initiative in Chad with Kenya's successful passage through this early stage. In early stages, donor initiatives cannot be expected to produce quick results; long-term commitment is essential, as the case of Kenya shows. These countries also need support in developing and implementing human resource strategies; in such areas as primary health care, education, employment, and gender equality, long-term improvements may be essential if family-size preferences are to decline and fertility regulation is to become more acceptable.

The political acceptability of fertility regulation in these countries is often difficult but also the most critical issue to address. Donor influence has to be used judiciously to increase political and public sensitivity to the health and

Box 6-3, continued

Kenya. The Bank first became involved in the population sector in Kenya in 1974, when public health services were relatively undeveloped. Two Bank projects, officially labeled population projects, were devoted largely to developing basic health infrastructure to support family planning efforts. At the same time the Bank provided considerable support for education, which took up 4 percent of lending—much more than in other regions—and financial assistance in such sectors as transport and communication. Not until the third population project in 1988 did the Bank focus narrowly on family planning systems. More recently, as other donors have sharply reduced their supplies of contraceptives, the Bank has begun to provide financing for this crucial component.

For more than a decade, fertility rates in Kenya stayed among the highest in the world, leading to negative assessments of earlier Bank projects. Finally, the 1989 Demographic and Health Survey documented, for the first time, a substantial, broad-based fertility decline, beginning in the early 1980s, probably triggered by a substantial expansion in service delivery points for family planning but also dependent on longer-term improvements in female education and declines in mortality (Kelley and Nobbe 1990). The 1993 Demographic and Health Survey documented an even more rapid decline of 20 percent in the last four years, to a total fertility rate of 5.4.

Kenya's incipient fertility transition has led to a reassessment of the earlier Bank projects. Their emphasis on social development and building basic infrastructure now appears to have been the right emphasis, and the long-term commitment of the Bank in population appears to have been essential (see World Bank 1992b).

---

welfare hazards of unrestrained reproduction. Equally important is the commitment to broader social policy, particularly in getting an early start on investments in education and addressing aspects of the legal and regulatory environment that restrict women's access to property, credit, and earnings opportunities.

Transitional Settings

Countries in the transitional stages of fertility decline face a broad range of conditions. The challenge for them, generally, is to continue to expand their clientele, which requires that they develop the infrastructure to support widespread services and maintain or expand political and popular support. The in-

BOX 6-4. EXAMPLES OF TRANSITIONAL SETTINGS

The diversity of country needs increases as countries move into the transitional phases of their fertility transitions, as Bank sector reviews and project experience indicate.

India. India was the very first country to adopt a national population policy and has the oldest and, with the possible exception of China, the largest national family planning program. India is also characterized by great regional diversity on both demographic and socioeconomic scales. Between 1970 and 1990, India's total fertility rate declined from about six to four births per woman. However, the national average masks fertility rates that are close to replacement level in several southern states but five or higher in poorer states in the north.

Despite much controversy and many reversals, India's family welfare program has succeeded in meeting the fertility regulation needs of about two-thirds of couples not desiring additional children. The program relies excessively on sterilization. Abortion is also widespread, and although abortion is legal, many abortions are per-formed under unsafe conditions. The family welfare program has done less well in addressing the needs of couples who wish to space births, and many demographers doubt whether India's demographic transition will complete itself unless a broader array of methods is made available (see World Bank 1992b).

A further weakness of India's population policy has been its narrow focus on demographic targets and neglect of broader social issues conducive to fertility decline. India has begun to re-assess its national population policy, and there has been increased discussion about how to develop a broader approach that will address issues such as the overall economic and social status of women and the neglect of investments in women's health. Several recent Bank projects are targeted on these problems, and further clarification of the nature of the Bank's long-standing involvement in the population field in India is expected to take place.

The Philippines. The Philippine family planning program was developed in the 1970s as a vertical initiative distinct from health but administered by the Department of Health. The initial focus

stitutional capacities they already have and the problems they face vary considerably. In some cases, the key groups for which services need to be extended may be poorly served rural populations; in others, they may be such special populations as adolescents. There may be cases where the main need is for outreach services; or there may be a need to achieve better integration with primary health care networks; still others may need to use private non-profit or commercial services more effectively. Box 6-4 provides illustrations

Box 6-4, continued

was strongly demographic. Policy changes, religious opposition, and dependence on external funding weakened the program in the early 1980s (see Russell and others 1991).

The Bank has supported a shift in emphasis to reproductive health concerns, emphasizing the health benefits of family planning (Casterline 1991). The national program is now premised partly on the risk to women and children's health caused by the absence of family planning: maternal mortality is estimated at 80 to 90 deaths per 100,000 live births, due mainly to complications of pregnancy. Another important premise of the program is respect for the rights of women who wish to regulate their fertility. The Bank has supported a client-oriented approach to services, ensuring the availability of contraceptive methods; strengthening information, education, and communication programming; supporting training; and improving program organization and management.

Iran. Recovering from the war with Iraq in the late 1980s, the government of Iran became increasingly disturbed by population growth rates exceeding 3 percent a year. A strong population policy was adopted and family planning services added to a well-designed primary health care system developed in the 1980s. The public response was enthusiastic, and contraceptive use rose significantly, while fertility fell (see Bulatao and Richardson 1993).

With demand for fertility regulation still strong, the Iranian family planning program faces various constraints. The contraceptive methods it provides have been biased toward those that are locally available but technically not always the most appropriate. Management of the family planning program, although adequate for the initial phase of program development, needs greater professionalism and technical expertise. Such program areas as information, education, communication, research, and evaluation are relatively undeveloped. With limited support from other donors, the program has worked with the Bank to launch a comprehensive project that attempts to deal with all these constraints.

of the range of issues that countries face during this transitional phase and the way the Bank has assessed and is trying to meet their needs.

Quality of care is a particularly important consideration in transitional settings. Poor quality, reflected in an inadequate mix of methods, poor counseling, and lack of courteous attention to clients, can have a particularly erosive effect at this stage (see Jain, Bruce, and Kumar 1992). In contrast, high-quality services often stimulate further demand as satisfied clients communicate their experiences by word of mouth. Method mix has implications for client satisfaction as well as the demographic effectiveness of programs. There is evidence in India, for example, that although sterilization is widely available, there is considerable unmet need for temporary methods to enable younger clients to delay or space births. In many districts, public sector clinics offering only sterilization are underused, while private clinics offering a full range of reproductive health services are generally busy, even when they charge for services.

Because the path from high to low fertility varies from country to country—and, as just noted, from region to region within countries—flexible strategies are required. In Bangladesh, for example, the Bank entered an unusual collaborative arrangement with other donors, in which the Bank tended to exercise its comparative advantage in the area of hardware provision, leaving the provision of much of the software components to other donors. At the same time, as borrower countries have themselves developed broader approaches to encompass the various new groups they must serve, the Bank has moved to provide software components that might enhance these efforts. This has put the Bank in a better position to support such initiatives as improving the quality and quantity of human resources, developing community outreach, facilitating the involvement of private voluntary organizations, increasing the range of contraceptive methods, reducing an excessive emphasis on sterilization, promoting breast-feeding and birth spacing, and increasing the attention given to gender issues and women's participation in development.

Advanced Settings

Replacement-level fertility has been achieved in some countries, especially in East Asia, through long-standing, very effective family planning programs coupled with substantial socioeconomic development. Nearly as low levels of fertility have been achieved in other countries with little if any national program effort. These two types of settings illustrate contrasting challenges. Where programs have successfully contributed to fertility reduction, the challenge may be to develop alternatives to public finance without jeopardizing current access to services. Where fertility has been reduced without benefit of an effective reproductive health system, the challenge is often twofold: to deal with inequity of access and provide services in poor, isolated communities; and to reduce reproductive health risks—from excessive dependence on abortion and poorly informed use of sometimes inappropriate contraceptive methods—that often develop in the absence of quality services. Box 6-5 gives two examples of countries that have advanced into low-fertility settings in which the absence of effective programs leaves many equity and health gaps.

Low-fertility countries also face a different set of demographic issues than countries at earlier stages of the transition process. Just as many of these countries have moved much more quickly through the transition from high to low fertility and mortality, so also are they experiencing more rapid shifts in age composition. Many developing countries are already expressing concerns about the aging of their populations, and new borrowers in Eastern Europe have been coping with a variety of complex demographic issues for a decade or more. Not only are their populations aging, but many are experiencing abrupt shifts in birth and death rates as a result of economic and political upheaval, and several are trying to cope with the relocation of ethnic groups affected by the realignment of national boundaries after the breakup of the former U.S.S.R.

Public and Private Sector Financing and Service Delivery

Developing countries differ greatly in the modalities they use both to finance and to provide reproductive health and family planning services. In the case of family planning, an estimated $5 billion was being spent annually on family planning in developing countries during the early 1990s. Of this total, around $3 billion came from developing-country governments, just over $1 billion from donors, and the remainder from payments by individual users. Just under $1 billion a year of the donor assistance came by way of grants, while the World Bank averaged an additional $200 million in loans and credits.

The overall level of donor assistance has grown over time. Figure 6-1 shows the levels of funding for the last decade in real and current terms. Real growth in global funding was quite rapid in the 1970s, slowed down in the 1980s, and picked up in the early 1990s. Population assistance is a small percentage—approximately 1 percent—of official development assistance. The ten major donor countries provided 97 percent of commitments to population assistance in 1991. They channeled approximately one-third of this assistance through multilateral agencies other than the World Bank and one-third through nongovernmental organizations over the three-year period from 1989 to 1991, according to available data on population assistance (see appendix A for a description of the international population assistance network).

Except in a few cases, it is difficult to disentangle expenditures on family planning from expenditures on the health programs with which they are often integrated. Although governments in the aggregate fund much greater proportions of their programs than do donors, regional variation is considerable. Governments fund the major part of the mature Asian programs. The government share of funding is somewhat lower (with more country-to-country variation) in Latin America, where nongovernmental organizations play a large

BOX 6-5. PROGRAM NEEDS IN
ADVANCED SETTINGS

Demographically advanced settings provide different challenges for programs. In some, such as in Singapore and the Republic of Korea, gradually phasing out the public role while maintaining wide access to services seems appropriate. In others, substantial problems still exist, as the cases of Brazil and Ukraine illustrate.

Brazil. The fertility rate in Brazil has declined significantly over the last twenty years, but contraceptives continue to be used ineffectively and often inappropriately. Sterilization is the main contraceptive method, and access to temporary methods is limited. Those who do use such temporary methods as the pill receive hardly any counseling and as a consequence have high failure rates. Contraceptive services vary widely in quality, and the public sector provides little support. In addition, rural women and the urban poor receive limited reproductive health services; approximately one in four women receive no prenatal care. The result is high maternal mortality, estimated to range, in urban areas, from 100 to 462 deaths per 100,000 live births. The majority of deaths are attributed to complications related to pregnancy and abortion (see Saxenian 1991).

To broaden access to reproductive health services, the Bank has assisted the Ministry of Health in developing or strengthening health infrastructure in rural and peri-urban areas. The Bank has focused attention on the need to

role—although with considerable financial support from donors, particularly during the early stages of their program development. Africa, for the most part, relies on public funding with donor support. In the Middle East and North Africa, the situation varies: in Tunisia and Morocco, governments provide the major proportion of funding, whereas in Egypt and Jordan, donors are the main source, although government financing is also considerable.

In general, only a small proportion of health budgets is allocated to family planning. Of the eighteen countries that can provide data for more than one year, half allotted less than 3 percent of their government health budgets to family planning. Five fell in the 3–10 percent range, three in the 10–18 percent range, and one in the 20–30 percent range.

Individual expenditures on family planning are estimated to amount to between 35 and 55 percent of what governments spend (World Bank 1993b). In the absence of public provision or subsidy of family planning, the amount that individuals would have to spend is substantial. In many low-income countries, the retail price of an annual supply of contraceptive pills, or of con-

expand the mix of methods and modify the dependence on cesarean sections as a pretext for sterilization: Brazil has one of the world's highest rates of cesarean sections. Given the way the private sector has filled some of the gaps left by public services, the Bank has also actively supported the integration of private services into the health network.

Ukraine. On becoming an independent country in 1991, Ukraine inherited a health care system in decay: overstaffed but lacking adequate emphasis on basic health services. Because of the very limited use of modern methods of contraception, Ukrainians depend heavily on abortion: the abortion ratio was 155 per 100 live births, or nearly 1 million abor-

tions a year. The negative impact on women's health was considerable: one-third of women who had abortions suffered from subsequent reproductive tract infections and as many as 60 percent experienced secondary sterility (see World Bank 1993d).

To reduce dependence on abortion, the Ministry of Health estimated that it would have to import about US$72 million in contraceptives, including intrauterine devices, birth control pills, and condoms. The Bank, making use in part of trust fund resources from Canada and Japan, is helping the ministry design a project to strengthen maternal and child health services in part by providing such essential contraceptive imports.

doms, would cost 5 percent of average annual income. In industrial countries, contraceptives seldom cost more than 1 percent of average income, even at much higher prices.

Not surprisingly, the pattern of use of services, available from demographic and health surveys, tends to mirror the patterns of financing described above. In Asia and Africa, where public financing tends to predominate, the source of provision tends to be government programs. In Latin America, where nongovernmental organizations play a larger role, generally speaking, the private sector plays a more significant role in service provision (see table 6-1).

The nature of private involvement in family planning often varies according to the type of contraceptive method being used. Pharmacies and other commercial outlets are more likely to be involved in distribution of resupply methods such as pills and condoms as opposed to clinical methods such as the intrauterine device or sterilization, which are typically provided by trained health workers in a clinical setting. Community-based distribution of nonclin-

Figure 6-1. International Population Assistance in Current U.S. Dollars, 1982–91

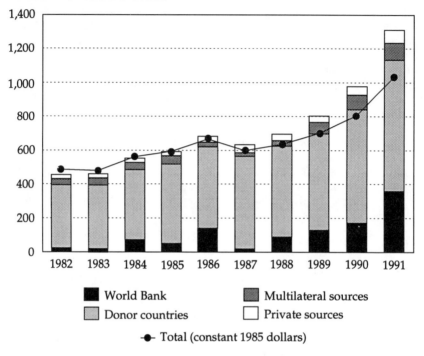

Millions of current U.S. dollars

Legend:
- ■ World Bank
- ▨ Multilateral sources
- ▨ Donor countries
- ☐ Private sources
- ●— Total (constant 1985 dollars)

a. Does not include contributions to United Nations Population Funds, to avoid double counting.
Source: UNFPA 1993a.

ical methods of contraception, a system now used in many government programs, was pioneered by nongovernmental organizations, which demonstrated its safety and effectiveness in extending services.

In the case of public/private partnerships, common variations are numerous. Private organizations often play an important role in testing new approaches, which are then used more widely in national programs. Many nongovernmental service providers are financed by the public sector or through international aid. Sometimes they operate from Ministry of Health clinics. Private hospitals and physicians that provide services receive reimbursements under government insurance schemes. In some instances, commercial providers receive public subsidies, as is the case in a number of contraceptive social marketing initiatives. The public sector also subcontracts to private

Table 6-1.   Sources of Modern Methods of Contraception in Countries with Contraceptive Prevalence over 30 Percent
(percentage)

Region	Contraceptive prevalence rate	Source Public sector	Source Private commercial	Source Private voluntary
Countries with per capita income below $1,000 a year				
Dominican Republic	47	42	48	1
Egypt	35	24	73	0
El Salvador	44	78	10	13
Honduras	33	19	25	52
Indonesia	50	76	22	0
Sri Lanka	40	85	8	2
Thailand	66	82	14	1
Zimbabwe	36	90	3	2
Average	44	62	25	9
Countries with per capita income above $1,000 a year				
Botswana	32	94	5	0
Brazil	56	28	69	1
Colombia	55	25	40	32
Ecuador	36	42	41	17
Mexico	45	63	36	0
Trinidad and Tobago	44	38	46	15
Tunisia	40	77	23	0
Average	44	52	37	9

Source: World Bank 1993b, table 10.

groups activities such as information and training. Several innovative approaches in the financing and provision of services have been introduced by the private sector, including employer-based insurance plans, provision of family planning by health maintenance organizations, and social marketing.

It is clear from table 6-1 that various patterns of public/private partnership have been successful in securing moderate to good contraceptive prevalence. The table also indicates that public provision has been important in several low-income settings, including Indonesia and Zimbabwe, where prevalence has reached the levels found in middle-income countries where private sources predominate. Even where the private sector is the main source, the public sector provides at least one-quarter of the services, providing a bedrock safety net for low-income clients.

The situation within countries also varies considerably. In Colombia, for example, where the nongovernmental organization Profamilia provides a major part of the country's contraceptive needs, the government plays a much greater role in the provision of services to users with little or no education and in rural areas than it does to groups with more education and in cities. (The commercial sector is the chief source for those with at least a secondary education.) Profamilia has moved away from dependence on donor assistance to increasing dependence on individual fees for payment; currently, it even provides some financial assistance to the public sector. Similar within-country differences in educational background are found between users of government and commercial sources of family planning in countries as diverse as Egypt, Jamaica, Morocco, Sri Lanka, and Thailand.

Estimating Resource Requirements

Borrowers have an interest in estimating the financial requirements of expanding family planning and reproductive health services to meet future needs. Estimating these amounts presents formidable difficulties. Two main approaches have been used to establish a baseline for these estimates. Both approaches rely on estimates of future levels of service provision if fertility decline follows the most likely projected path. One approach starts with estimates of expenditures in the sector, divides them by the number of people being served, and then projects them into the future. The second approach estimates current unit costs of providing family planning and multiplies them by the current and projected number of users. Both approaches adjust for inflation and other factors that are likely to influence cost or expenditure levels in the future (for example, the level of institutional capacity and the stage of program development in a country). In fact, both methods yield broadly similar estimates when they are stated in per capita terms. A compilation of estimates reviewed in the recent Bank paper on best practices in family planning indicates that per capita expenditures, including user payments, will remain modest at $1.25 to $1.50 a year. *World Development Report 1993* reports a similar figure, estimating that family planning could be provided at a cost of about $0.90 per capita in low-income countries and $2.20 per capita in middle-income countries (World Bank 1993e).

The growing consensus that safe and effective fertility regulation is central to reproductive health has prompted efforts to estimate what it would cost to provide a minimum package of interventions in this area. The Bank's estimates of the cost of a safe motherhood program (excluding child health) range between $0.92 and $1.06 per capita, again assuming different levels of development. These estimates attribute only a portion of the costs of family planning services to safe motherhood interventions and include the costs of contraceptives at a public sector instead of a commercial price.

Costing information for these more comprehensive packages is still limited. Available estimates of the costs of family planning services do not include management of abortions or control and prevention of HIV/AIDS and reproductive tract infections, both essential elements of reproductive health. In addition, a population program more broadly defined would include the costs of ancillary activities—for example, censuses, registration systems, surveys, and the institutions necessary to conduct and analyze them and to advise on policy. How to apportion joint costs and what to include in costing population programs are important issues with no "correct" solutions, but consistency is crucial to dependable estimates of resource needs.

Although the per capita costs of providing reproductive health and family planning services are not expected to increase greatly, the total costs will increase considerably because of the increasing numbers of men and women of reproductive age and the expanded use of these services by currently underserved groups. To cover these costs it is estimated that expenditures on family planning services will have to increase by 55 to 60 percent over the decade (World Bank 1993b). Harder to estimate is the added expense as programs broaden their coverage to other aspects of reproductive health, but it is likely to be considerable. In its preparations for the 1994 population conference, the United Nations Population Fund estimated that at the global level a doubling of expenditures (from around $5 billion to just over $10 billion in 1993 dollars) will be required to meet family planning needs, plus an added $5 billion–$7 billion to address broader reproductive health needs (UNFPA 1994). The estimates are imprecise because countries differ greatly in the amount of capital investments they require and in the level of local recurrent costs.

Reproductive health and family planning services require modest investments in comparison with countries' other health and development needs. Public financing and service provision should be targeted on underserved groups, the poor in particular. In some countries, the needs for expanded information and services could be met by a reallocation of public expenditures away from activities that could be addressed better by the private sector. The poorest developing countries' governments may not have sufficient resources to finance and to provide the services to meet these needs. Donors can play a role, but there are also limits to what they may be able to provide. In all cases, attention needs to be given to efficiency gains in the provision of services, including those that derive from involvement of private providers, and to mechanisms to recover costs or provide services through commercial channels in situations where users are able to pay for them.

CHAPTER SEVEN

Implications for the World Bank

W ORLD Bank involvement in population has changed over time to reflect not only a growing understanding of the complexity of the linkages between population and development but also an awareness that many factors affect reproductive behavior. The Bank recognizes that other investments in human development affect the desire for smaller families, in particular girls' education, and has consequently also been addressing this dimension. The Bank's approach also reflects a conviction that reproductive health and family planning are important components of better health for mothers and children and of family and women's rights. As the Bank has sharpened its focus on poverty reduction, investments in human resource development, and sustainable economic growth, population is being viewed increasingly in terms of its relevance to these prime goals.

The Bank's Comparative Advantages

The World Bank's role in population programs has been shaped by its comparative advantage in a number of areas in relation to the many multilateral, bilateral, and nongovernmental organizations that are involved in population work (see appendix A for a description of the international population assistance network). Although the Bank is not the lead agency in population, it has played an increasingly important role as it has responded to borrower demands. Bank managers and staff have increased their capacity to work with borrowers, other donors, and nongovernmental organizations to formulate effective projects to meet the diverse needs that have been identified in this review. However, Bank capacity to respond to borrower demand should be strengthened further and is an important issue for continued expansion of population and social sector work.

The Bank helps borrowers address population through a broad range of social sector interventions, including health, education, and the status of women. The Bank also brings particular strength in sector and economic analyses, which inform the policy dialogue between the Bank and borrower countries. Bank resources, although available through loans and credits to borrowers, are usually available on a more ample scale than nonreimbursed funds from other donors. The Bank's sectoral and lending approach encourages borrowers, in formulating their projects, to look comprehensively at sector needs and to take action to resolve issues and achieve clearly identifiable goals that are consistent with overall development objectives.

Other donors offer grants, which are often a more attractive funding mechanism for population programs than are loans, and they provide a wider and deeper range of technical assistance at the field level. Those donors may have greater flexibility in providing direct support to nongovernmental organizations, which have tended to be the more innovative and energetic organizations in the area of family planning, while the Bank must deal primarily with governments, and in the case of population, typically with ministries (health and/or family welfare), which often are not the most powerful public agencies. For the remainder of this chapter, the prime focus is on the reproductive health and family planning aspects of the population program, with a number of general cross-references to health and education. More detailed analyses of education and health activities can be found in other Bank documents.

Policy Dialogue and Analytical Work

High-level understanding and political commitment have been very important elements of successful population work. The Bank has participated in this policy development process through its dialogue with borrowers, drawing not only on its sectoral expertise but also on the economic skills that contribute to its comparative advantage in policy development. Although the impact of sector work on policy is hard to measure, the Bank is generally credited with contributing to policy breakthroughs in a number of countries, particularly in Asia and in Sub-Saharan Africa, where the Bank put major emphasis on population growth issues during the 1980s. These efforts contributed to the broad policy changes observed there during the last decade (see box 7-1) and led to substantial increases in the lending program. In other countries, Bank sector

---

BOX 7-1. POLICY DIALOGUE IN SUB-SAHARAN AFRICA

During the 1980s the World Bank engaged Africa leadership groups—top government officials, administrators, academics, and opinion leaders—in a dialogue on the linkages between rapid population growth and the development prospects of the region. The main messages are presented in a World Bank Policy Study, *Population* *Growth and Policies in Sub-Saharan Africa* (World Bank 1986). That study drew on extensive sector work, which was later published in *Population Growth and Reproduction in Sub-Saharan Africa* (Acsadi, Johnson-Acsadi, and Bulatao 1990). Follow-up to this effort was carried out by the African Population Advisory Committee, a group of distinguished experts and leaders in African population and development issues (see APAC 1993).

---

work has played a supporting role in the development of population policies, although this has not resulted in projects financed by the Bank.

Analysis of demographic issues in reports that concentrate on population is generally strong. As population has become increasingly integrated within population, health, and nutrition projects, or as part of a larger social sector initiative, population work has been integrated within those larger reports. For example, a recent review of women in development issues in Niger addresses interrelations between reproductive behavior, rural production, and management of natural resources (see Bach-Baouab 1993). Several education and health reports have identified alternative policy options needed to respond to different patterns of change in the age structure of populations. A population perspective has also been incorporated in other sector work (agriculture, labor, and poverty), drawing attention, for example, to increases in the number of people in poverty and the association between family size and family poverty.

However, as some critics have noted, opportunities to bring population more fully into the policy dialogue have been missed by not giving sufficient attention to demographic trends and their implications in country strategies and economic analyses (see Teitelbaum 1989 and appendix C for a synopsis of other reviews of Bank population work). To enable the Bank to do a better job in assessing population issues, more targeted training and better guidance on population issues for country economists and senior managers are being undertaken, along with efforts to encourage more systematic incorporation of demographic issues in country strategies and economic analyses.

Bank-sponsored research provides the analytical basis for policy dialogue and lending operations. A wide variety of studies has focused on individual and household decisionmaking with respect to demographic variables, look-

ing at a range of issues such as the relative cost-effectiveness of efforts to reduce fertility through reductions in infant and child mortality, increases in
family planning, or increases in female education. For example, a recent series of studies has addressed economic and policy determinants of fertility in
Sub-Saharan Africa, with particular emphasis on how investments among various social sectors affect reproductive behavior (see Scribner 1994). At the
same time, less attention has been directed to several issues of increasing policy importance at the Bank: international migration, aging, and the environmental consequences of population growth. Important exceptions are *World
Development Report 1984* and a follow-up study on the links between population growth, environment, and agriculture in Africa. Likewise, little recent
work has been done on the effects of fertility decisions on poverty, although
important studies were done earlier in Indonesia and Botswana during preparations for *World Development Report 1984*. More recently, research on the
interrelations between population growth and natural resource use has become
a growing focus of attention, as exemplified in *World Development Report
1992: Development and the Environment*. As the Bank addresses the question
of how to do a better job in bringing the demographic perspective into its
country work, it will need to expand its base of knowledge about the linkages
between demographic variables and its core interests in poverty reduction, human resource development, and environmentally sustainable development.

Trends in Lending

Over the past twenty-five years, the Bank has been an active player in the
population field, lending more than $1.7 billion to support population activ-
ities through more than 100 projects. As figure 7-1 demonstrates, the value of
the total portfolio[1] has increased steadily, reaching $50 million in fiscal 1973,
$295 million in fiscal 1983, and a current (fiscal 1993) value of more than $1.1
billion, representing seventy-three projects under Bank supervision (either
free-standing population projects or health and social development projects in
which family planning is a significant component). Although new commitments vary considerably by year, here too the trend has been steadily upward.
In the first decade of Bank involvement (1969–79), eighteen free-standing
population projects were approved, worth almost $300 million. In fiscal 1980–
87, twenty-seven population-related projects were approved, with the amount
financing population activities estimated at about $425 million. In the period
since fiscal 1988, sixty-three projects supporting population activities have
been approved by the board, providing more than $1 billion in support. In the
1990s, new commitments have averaged about $200 million a year.[2]

Historically, the principal beneficiaries of Bank lending in population

Figure 7-1.   World Bank Lending to Population: Continuing Portfolio and Annual Commitments, Fiscal Years 1970–93

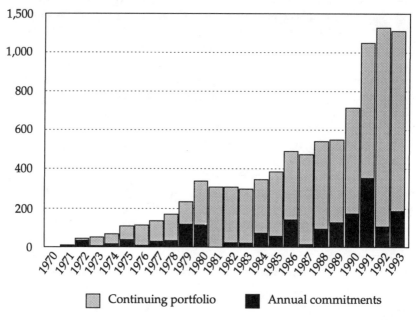

Millions of current U.S. dollars

☐ Continuing portfolio   ■ Annual commitments

Source: Data from the World Bank, Management Information System and Population, Health, and Nutrition Department.

have been in Asia. Between them, East and South Asia have received almost 70 percent of the Bank's total support to population, with Bangladesh, India, and Indonesia accounting for more than half of the total. The focus on Asia has been motivated by many factors, including its large and rapidly growing population (more than half the world's population lives in Asia) and the political commitment of leaders in these countries. These projects have tended to be large and free-standing, although the last five years have seen more integrated projects.

Although Asia has received the most population financing, Africa has had a greater number of projects. In contrast to the situation in Asia, these projects are mostly integrated population, health, and nutrition projects, whose population activities account for almost 20 percent of total population lending, the next largest proportion after the two Asian regions. The countries of the Middle East and North Africa have historically received very little lending for population. The last three years, however, have seen an increase in activity. Aside from the new Europe and Central Asia region, the countries of the Latin America and Caribbean region have received the smallest proportion of Bank population resources because of political sensitivities and the predominance of other donors. In this region, although there is little Bank activity in the population area, integrated population, health, and nutrition projects often include components related to family planning, and social investment funds are available for support of family planning (see figure 7-2).

The amounts shown in figures 7-1 and 7-2 provide only a partial picture of the Bank's true contribution to the sector; they reflect efforts to increase the *supply* of family planning services. They do not include funding that supports fertility reduction by increasing the *demand* for smaller families. Three sets of interventions are especially effective in creating such demand: those that improve health and reduce infant mortality; those that improve access to education, particularly for girls; and, most fundamentally, those that are meant to reduce poverty and raise income levels.

In health the Bank is involved in a wide range of activities that contribute in various ways to fertility reduction and that, in fiscal 1993, amounted to approximately $1.6 billion in new commitments (this excludes the $186 million assigned above to population components). For example, fifty-five projects with substantial AIDS/HIV prevention and treatment activities have been approved, most of which are currently under supervision. Similarly, at the end of fiscal 1993, more than seventy projects with safe motherhood components were under implementation. In addition, the Bank funds a number of child survival interventions, which (like safe motherhood) contribute to the broader reproductive health objectives described in chapter 6.

Bank investments in education (which amounted to $1.9 billion in fiscal 1993) are increasingly being targeted on keeping girls in school. The objective is to raise the value of women as producers rather than as child bearers and to help reduce their dependence on their husbands and sons, which affects the desire for large numbers of children. Strategies to target discrete groups (especially women and the poor) and to help them take better advantage of educational opportunities have been coupled with efforts to increase the capability of local institutions to provide quality education and reproductive health services. In fiscal 1993, about 45 percent of all approved Bank projects contained gender-specific interventions. In the population, health, and nutrition sector, that figure jumped to 90 percent; in employment and training, to 83 percent; and in education, to 67 percent.

Figure 7-2. Value and Composition of the Population Portfolio, Fiscal Years 1970–93

Millions of current U.S. dollars

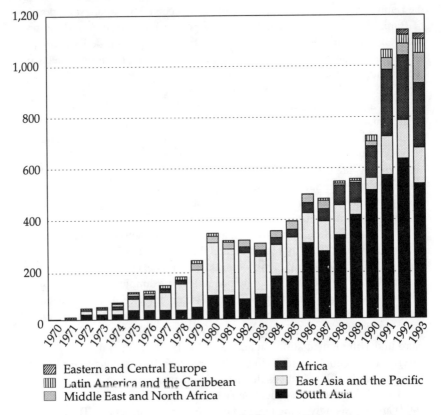

Eastern and Central Europe

Latin America and the Caribbean

Middle East and North Africa

Africa

East Asia and the Pacific

South Asia

Note: A project is included in the portfolio for a given year if it was approved before or during and closed during or after that fiscal year.

Source: Data from the World Bank Management Information System and Population, Health, and Nutrition Department.

Factors Influencing the Effectiveness of Population Projects

The population activities of the Bank are influenced by many factors, including its role in relation to other donors, institutional capacities of client countries, and the complex nature of the field. This section reviews those issues and briefly describes how the Bank has been addressing them.

Loans/Credits versus Grants

The Bank's status as a lending institution allows it to work on a larger scale than most other donors, whose work in population is through grants. Within the health sector, the Bank can mobilize large sums of money to build the health system infrastructure. Further, its multisectoral approach enables it to lend in fields that reinforce investment in family planning, such as education and health. However, its status as a bank limits the size of its lending program in cases where the need for hardware is less than the need for software or where institutional capacity to manage large-scale projects is weak. However, well-structured projects often leverage financing from other donors for items such as contraceptive supplies.

Some of these limitations are attenuated when countries qualify for credits through the International Development Association (IDA), which offers borrowers more attractive terms than are available in the case of loans made by the International Bank for Reconstruction and Development (IBRD).[3] More than 70 percent of the Bank's lending for population has been in the form of IDA credits. When projects are financed with IBRD loans, countries are likely to prefer civil works and other hardware activities, particularly those requiring foreign exchange. When projects are financed with IDA credits, more of the software needs of this sector (training, motivational activities, and contraceptive supply and logistics systems) are likely to be included. In IDA-eligible countries, the Bank also finances a higher proportion of project costs (up to 90 percent). However, because IDA credits are available only to low-income countries, it is more difficult to finance activities in poorer regions of countries not otherwise qualifying. There is strong support among IDA-10 donors for increased population work by the Bank, and the IDA-10 agreement calls on the Bank to increase its investments further in this area.

Institutional Capacity

Operating as a lending agency also means that the Bank does not implement projects. Implementation is the responsibility of the borrower, normally government departments and generally the Ministry of Health in the case of population. Although the Bank has supervisory responsibilities, it does not manage project activities. Furthermore, the implementing agency can be the beneficiary under the loan agreement, but foreign exchange must be disbursed under arrangements with ministries of finance and central banks that the implementing agency cannot control. Delays and bureaucratic tie-ups in the flow-through of funds can sometimes stall project activities. Although this is a general issue for Bank projects, the relatively weak position of many ministries of health in many countries makes it particularly severe in this sector.

Complexity

As the Bank responds to current changes in the population environment—the increased diversity of client needs and the trend toward a more integrated approach—it is also being required to develop projects that combine a greater variety of components and cofinancing mechanisms. This complexity raises the time costs for analysis and project formulation and places greater demands on the institutional capacity of borrower countries to implement those projects.

Supervision and Skill Mix

Investing in the social sectors is labor intensive and requires specialized technical and organizational skills; for reasons indicated above, population offers additional challenges, particularly in the supervision of projects. Some of the Bank's more successful population and health projects have, in fact, included provision for resident management staff to strengthen supervisory capacity (for example, in Bangladesh and Kenya). The experience of other donors also suggests a strong relationship between the intensity of in-country management efforts and the effectiveness of projects. The Bank has been making a special effort to improve supervision and strengthen its skill mix in needed technical areas and to assure that it is responsive to borrowers' needs. It is also exploring mechanisms for drawing more effectively on technical expertise in specialized United Nations agencies such as United Nations Population Fund and World Health Organization.

Increasing Involvement of Nongovernmental Organizations

In view of the growing belief that institutions with strong links to local communities are more sustainable and lead to productive use of resources in the long term, many donors are looking to nongovernmental organizations to act as intermediaries between them and the communities they wish to serve. This is happening despite some reservations about their relative cost-effectiveness as service providers; some argue that even donated resources should be assigned an economic cost when allocation decisions are being made. The accumulated technical expertise and experience with service delivery of nongovernmental organizations is of paramount importance to the Bank. Also, success in population projects depends to a large extent on the quality of relations between providers and clients. A growing number of Bank projects involves such organizations, particularly national organizations with a commitment to community service, especially where clients are geographically or socially disadvantaged. The highly differentiated nature of client populations and the organizational context within which public family planning services are offered make nongovernmental organizations a promising alternative mechanism for channeling Bank investments.

Donor Coordination

Another way to enhance the Bank's effectiveness in population is to find new opportunities for donor coordination. The Bank's work in population has already benefited from considerable donor coordination, both at the level of country programs and at the international level. Cofinancing by governments and other donors at the country level led to total project cost support to population in fiscal 1993 that was twice as large as the Bank lending figure. In the case of the Zimbabwe Second Family Health Project approved in fiscal 1991, the Bank mobilized $17.7 million in grant funds for population, leaving no need for Bank lending for population components of that project. Similar examples include the Cameroon and the Gambia population, health, and nutrition projects approved in fiscal 1990.

Perhaps more important than the amount of cofinancing, however, is the content of the coordination activities. The Bangladesh Population and Health Consortium is an excellent example of effective donor coordination in which Bank-sponsored projects include large amounts of grant assistance (more than two-thirds of the external funding), allowing for larger expenditures on technical assistance, fellowships and training, and operating costs than is typical in Bank projects. Grant funds also paid for additional staff both in the field and in Washington, D.C., to supervise the project, provide policy guidance, and coordinate donor efforts. In this and other cases, the greater field presence of other population agencies could be capitalized on to overcome some of the constraints on the Bank's own effectiveness, such as limited staff resources for supervision, hesitation of clients to borrow for software, and limited institutional capacity of some borrowers.

The Bank's Role in Meeting the Challenges of the 1990s and Beyond

In response to the challenges reviewed above, the Bank's capacity in policy dialogue and resource mobilization is its most effective tool. The Bank will continue to use and strengthen its sector work and policy dialogue to urge governments to examine demographic issues in light of other development priorities and to make funding allocations as appropriate. The Bank will also draw borrowers' attention to the many modalities available for funding and providing services and identify and urge changes in constraints on access to family planning information and methods. It will point out that public policy can encourage or inhibit private sector work in population and it will encourage borrowers to address legal and regulatory constraints, such as limits or restrictions on the importation of contraceptives, price controls, limits on the flow of information in the sector, and overly restrictive reporting and oversight standards.

The Bank will also continue to help borrowers understand and build on the broader linkages between population change and other aspects of human development and poverty reduction. Through its own investments in health and education, and by encouraging borrowers and other donors to put high priority on these areas, the Bank will help borrowers reduce high rates of maternal and child mortality, bridge the gender gap in education, and raise women's economic and social status. These investments will speed up fertility declines. They are beneficial in their own right, and they should be accorded high priority for both reasons.

In sum, the Bank will emphasize the following:

- Working with borrower countries and other donors to mobilize financial and other resources required to meet the growing demand for family planning, reproductive health services, education, and other services that contribute to human development
- Assisting borrower countries through its own strategic investments in these sectors, with emphasis on infrastructure, institutional capacity, and effective management of sector activities
- Coordinating the mobilization of resources as much as possible with efforts to supply the core package of essential health services called for in *World Development Report 1993* and applying that report's guidance on health finance and management in working with borrowers on family planning and reproductive health projects
- Strengthening the Bank's skill mix in needed technical areas, applying its available capacity for financial and economic analysis in the sector, and working collaboratively with other donors and specialized agencies that have complementary skills and capacities, and
- Using its analytical capacity and supporting research to broaden the scope of population policy through better understanding of the linkages between population change, reproductive health,

and the Bank's broader human development and poverty
alleviation agendas, and recognizing more effectively in
country strategies and other key documents the interconnections
between population dynamics and successful achievement of
those agendas.

Ultimately, the needs, implementation capacities, and commitment to
policy reform of borrowing countries will determine the volume and content
of the Bank's social sector lending. For its part, the Bank expects to sustain
and expand its recent efforts to work with borrowers in developing and implementing a larger and more comprehensive program in human resource development. Over the Bank's three-year planning horizon, sector work in the areas
of education and population, health, and nutrition is projected to continue to
expand, with an emphasis on completing poverty assessments for all borrowers and improving sector knowledge in support of increased investment.
Bank management is committed to a larger program of investment in family
planning, maternal and child health, and increased educational opportunities
for girls. Although detailed lending projections are subject to considerable uncertainties, present lending plans indicate that the recent growth of social sector lending will be sustained over the planning period. Lending for reproductive health and family planning activities is projected to increase by 50
percent over the next three years, the annual total of lending for health is projected to exceed $2 billion for the first time in fiscal 1996, and lending for
education is expected to average more than $2.5 billion in fiscal 1995–97
(with a substantial emphasis on girls' education), provided that country environments are supportive of policy reform and effective implementation.

Notes

1. A project is included in the portfolio for a given year if it was approved
before or during and closed during or after that fiscal year. This definition is
consistent with the Bank's annual review of portfolio performance (World
Bank 1994c).

2. Integration of population with health and nutrition activities makes the
method of accounting for dollar amounts supporting population activities an
inexact science at best and has led to a very restrictive definition of what is
counted as "population" to avoid double counting among the subsectors. The
operating definition for population lending is activities that provide direct and
indirect support of family planning service delivery, population policy development, and fertility survey/census work. This definition understates the
Bank's true contribution to the sector in several ways. It does not include di-

rectly related activities of service provision such as prevention and treatment of AIDS and sexually transmitted diseases, nor does it include the nonfamily planning elements of safe motherhood programs and child survival interventions, both of which are now considered part of the population and reproductive health field. Appendix B provides a more detailed discussion of how the annual amounts of population lending are counted in the Bank and lists Bank projects that have population components as well as the total amount and the amount allocated for population.

3. IBRD was established in 1945 to help finance reconstruction and development in member countries. IDA was established in 1960 to provide assistance to the poorest developing countries on terms that would bear less heavily on the balance of payments than IBRD loans. Only the very poorest countries are eligible for IDA credits, which, when discounted over the length of the credit period, represent an 88 percent grant equivalent. At present the rate of interest on IBRD loans is about 7.5 percent, with a grace period of five years and a repayment period of fifteen to twenty years. IDA credits have a ten-year grace period and must be repaid in thirty-five or forty years.

APPENDIX A

The International Population Assistance Network

INTERNATIONAL population assistance flows from developed-country donors to developing-country governments and nongovernmental organizations both directly and indirectly through a network of multilateral agencies and international nongovernmental organizations. The United Nations Population Fund (UNFPA) conducts periodic reviews of international assistance, with the most recent one covering the period 1982–91 (UNFPA 1993a). As noted in chapter 7 of the report, donor assistance to population increased steadily during the 1980s when measured in current dollars. For the three-year period 1989–91, the total amount of commitments for population assistance from the seventeen developed-country governments that responded to the UNFPA inquiry averaged $670 million dollars (see table A-1). The twelve countries listed in the table, headed by the United States with $294 million, accounted for almost all (97 percent) of that amount.

This assistance flows through a variety of channels, including United Nations agencies and international nongovernmental organizations. Figure A-1, prepared by UNFPA, presents a stylized depiction of these channels. About one-third of overall assistance goes directly from developed- to developing-country governments in the form of bilateral assistance. The United States channels the largest share, 55 percent, of its assistance in the form of bilateral aid. Other countries that channel much of their assistance bilaterally are Germany (38 percent) and Canada (37 percent).

Another third of developing-country government assistance is channeled

Table A-1. Developed-Country Commitments to Population Assistance, by Channel and as a Percentage of Official Development Assistance and Gross National Product, Averages for 1989–91

Country	Total (thousands of U.S. dollars)	Percentage channeled through			As a percentage of	
		Direct bilateral aid	Multilateral organizations	Nongovernmental organizations	Official development assistance	Gross national product
United States	293,586	55	0	45	2.94	0.005
Japan	62,310	10	65	24	0.65	0.002
Germany, Fed. Republic of	53,946	38	52	9	0.88	0.004
Norway	49,179	22	61	16	4.49	0.050
Sweden	39,876	4	58	38	2.01	0.020
United Kingdom	37,375	24	39	37	1.31	0.004
Netherlands	35,742	10	81	9	1.50	0.014
Canada	34,711	37	37	26	1.41	0.006
Denmark	21,334	2	73	25	1.94	0.018
Finland	20,906	2	96	2	2.50	0.015
Switzerland	6,182	6	93	1	0.86	0.003
Australia	5,361	24	52	24	0.53	0.002
Others[a]	9,702	17	72	11	0.17	0.001
Total	670,210	34	34	32	1.25	0.009

a. Averaged less than $5 million a year each, including Austria, Belgium, France, Italy, and New Zealand.
Source: UNFPA 1994, unpublished addendum.

through multilateral agencies, including the UNFPA, World Health Organization, United Nations Children's Fund, and other United Nations agencies. These agencies made grants either to developing countries' governments or to national nongovernmental organizations in developing countries. Most developed-country governments, including Australia, Denmark, Finland, Germany, Japan, Netherlands, Norway, Sweden, and Switzerland, channel half or more of their population assistance through multilateral agencies. The United States, which did not channel any assistance through multilateral channels from 1986 to 1992, resumed funding through them in 1993. The World Bank's commitments to population activities, which averaged $215 million for 1989–91, are not included in the flows channeled through multilateral agencies because only part of its funding in this sector can be said to originate in contributions (through IDA) from developed-country governments.

The other main channel for international population assistance consists of international private organizations, which received funding from both developed-country governments and from private foundations in developed countries. Some thirty-seven international nongovernmental organizations responded to the most recent UNFPA inquiry; they reported that they had received income from an additional 113 international nongovernmental organizations and that they had channeled amounts to an additional 286 international and 105 national nongovernmental organizations in developing countries.

Private organizations are an important source of funding for international nongovernmental organizations. The largest six, all based in the United States, accounted for 62 percent of the $54 million in annual private assistance to nongovernmental organizations over the three-year period 1989–91; they include the Rockefeller Foundation, the MacArthur Foundation, the Population Council, the Hewlett Foundation, the Ford Foundation, and the Mellon Foundation.

Several developed-country donors channel a portion of their population assistance through international nongovernmental organizations. Slightly less than one-third of developed-country government assistance flows in this way. Sweden, the United Kingdom, and the United States channel more than a third (38, 37, and 45 percent, respectively) of their assistance through international nongovernmental organizations. Five international nongovernmental organizations accounted for nearly three-fourths of the assistance flowing in this way: the International Planned Parenthood Federation, the Population Council, the Association of Voluntary Surgical Sterilization, the Program for Appropriate Technology in Health, and Pathfinder International. Most of these larger international nongovernmental organizations play a dual role as channels of international assistance and as sources of funding, so that the Population Council, for example, is listed as being one of the largest private sources as well as private channels of funding.

Accounting for Bank Spending in Population

THE growing diversity and complexity of Bank work in population and related health and social development activities have increased the difficulty of providing a satisfactory dollar accounting for the "population" component of these activities. Early stand-alone population projects of the 1970s were generally counted as 100 percent population, even though they actually included lending for health infrastructure and other elements that might be considered health or nutrition. This definition was appropriate, because the major objective of the projects was to accelerate fertility decline and the Bank was not yet officially lending for health per se. As the public, health, and nutrition sector became more integrated during the 1980s, the Bank's management information system did not formally distinguish between the population, health, and nutrition components of projects. Nor were clients required to provide information on the allocation of disbursements among these components.

For a variety of reasons, there is considerable interest in assigning identifiable dollar amounts to population as well as to other project components. One of these is the desire of advocacy groups to have a number to use in judging the adequacy of donor funding of population activities. Therefore, Bank staff prepare estimates of these amounts on a project-by-project basis using appraisal reports submitted to the board for approval. Because other subsectoral advocates are also interested in claiming amounts for their areas of interest and because Bank management has directed that there be no double counting of subsectoral components, what currently gets counted as population in Bank lending operations is more narrowly defined than in the past. It is

Table B-1. World Bank's Projects Supporting Population Activities

Loan/credit	Fiscal year	Region[a]	Country	Project name	Lending amount (millions)	Amount for population programs (millions)
L	1970	LA	Jamaica	Family planning	2.0	2.0
L	1971	LA	Trinidad and Tobago	Family planning	3.0	3.0
C	1971	MN	Tunisia	Population	4.8	4.8
C	1972	EA	Indonesia	Population I	13.2	13.2
C	1972	SA	India	Population	21.1	21.1
L	1973	EA	Malaysia	Population	5.0	5.0
C	1974	AF	Kenya	Population I	12.0	12.0
C	1974	MN	Egypt	Population	4.8	4.8
L	1975	EA	Philippines	Population	25.0	25.0
C	1975	SA	Bangladesh	Population I	15.0	15.0
L	1976	LA	Jamaica	Population II and nutrition	6.8	6.8
L	1977	EA	Indonesia	Population II	24.5	24.5
L	1977	LA	Dominican Republic	Family welfare	5.0	5.0
C	1978	EA	Thailand	Population I	33.1	33.1

(Table continues on the following page)

115

Table B-1 *(continued)*

Loan/ credit	Fiscal year	Region[a]	Country	Project name	Lending amount (millions)	Amount for population programs (millions)
L	1979	EA	Malaysia	Population II	17.0	17.0
C	1979	EA	Philippines	Population II	40.0	40.0
C	1979	MN	Egypt	Population II	25.0	25.0
C	1979	SA	Bangladesh	Population II	32.0	32.0
L	1980	EA	Indonesia	Population III	35.0	35.0
L	1980	EA	Korea, Republic of	Population I	30.0	30.0
C	1980	SA	India	Population II	46.0	46.0
L	1981	MN	Tunisia	Health and population	12.5	1.1
C	1982	AF	Kenya	Population II	23.0	23.0
C	1983	AF	Senegal	Rural health	15.0	1.4
C	1983	AF	Malawi	Health and nutrition	6.8	0.6
L	1983	LA	Peru	Health	33.5	1.0
C	1983	SA	Pakistan	Population	18.0	18.0
C	1984	AF	Mali	Health development	16.7	1.5
L	1984	AF	Botswana	Family health	11.0	0.8
C	1984	AF	Comoros	Population and health	2.8	0.4
C	1984	SA	India	Population III	70.0	70.0

C	AF	1985	Lesotho	Health and population	3.5	0.7
C	AF	1985	Burkina Faso	Health I	26.6	0.5
L	AF	1985	Nigeria	Sokoto health	34.0	1.4
L	EA	1985	Indonesia	Population IV	46.0	46.0
L	MN	1985	Jordan	Health	13.5	3.4
L	MN	1985	Morocco	Health development	28.4	2.8
C	AF	1986	Sierra Leone	Population and health	5.3	1.1
C	AF	1986	Rwanda	Family health	10.8	1.2
L	AF	1986	Côte d'Ivoire	Health I	22.2	4.9
C	AF	1986	Niger	Health	27.8	1.7
C	AF	1986	Ghana	Health and education rehabilitation	15.0	0.8
L	LA	1986	Colombia	Public health	36.5	0.3
C	SA	1986	India	West Bengal population	51.0	51.0
C	SA	1986	Bangladesh	Population III	78.0	78.0
C	AF	1987	Guinea-Bissau	Population, health, and nutrition	4.2	0.5
C	AF	1987	Gambia	Population and health	5.6	0.6
L	AF	1987	Zimbabwe	Family health	10.0	2.0
C	AF	1987	Malawi	Health and population II	11.0	4.8
L	LA	1987	Jamaica	Population and health I	10.0	6.8
C	AF	1988	Burundi	Health and population I	14.0	4.4
C	AF	1988	Ethiopia	Family health	33.0	3.3
C	AF	1988	Kenya	Population III	12.2	22.2
C	SA	1988	India	Bombay and Madras population	57.0	57.0
C	SA	1988	Sri Lanka	Health and population	17.5	5.3

(Table continues on the following page)

Table B-1 (continued)

Loan/credit	Fiscal year	Region[a]	Country	Project name	Lending amount (millions)	Amount for population programs (millions)
L	1989	AF	Nigeria	State health and population	27.6	0.1
C	1989	AF	Benin	Health services development	18.6	0.3
C	1989	MN	Yemen	Health II	4.5	0.4
C	1989	SA	India	Family welfare training	124.6	124.6
C	1990	AF	Kenya	Population IV	35.0	35.0
C	1990	AF	Lesotho	Health and population II	12.1	1.2
C	1990	AF	Tanzania	Health and nutrition	47.6	9.5
C	1990	LA	Haiti	Health and population	28.2	1.6
L	1990	LA	Brazil	Northeast basic health II	267.0	13.4
C	1990	MN	Yemen	Health II	15.0	1.5
L	1990	MN	Morocco	Health sector investment	104.0	10.4
C	1990	SA	India	Population training VII	96.7	96.7
C	1991	AF	Senegal	Human resources I (population and health)	35.0	14.8
C	1991	AF	Rwanda	Population	19.6	19.6
C	1991	AF	Nigeria	Population	78.5	78.5
C	1991	AF	Togo	Population and health adjustment	14.2	4.3
C	1991	AF	Madagascar	National health sector	31.0	4.4
C	1991	AF	Malawi	PHN sector credit	55.5	5.8
C	1991	AF	Mali	Health, population, and rural welfare	26.6	3.0

C	1991	AF	Ghana	Health and population II	27.0	4.9
L	1991	EA	Indonesia	Population V	104.0	104.0
L	1991	LA	Venezuela	Social development	100.0	5.0
C	1991	LA	Haiti	Economic and social fund	11.3	0.5
C	1991	LA	Honduras	Social fund	20.0	0.2
L	1991	LA	El Salvador	Social sector rehabilitation	26.0	1.5
L	1991	LA	Mexico	Basic health	180.0	3.5
L	1991	MN	Tunisia	Population and family health	26.0	26.0
C	1991	SA	Pakistan	Family health	45.0	13.5
C	1991	SA	Bangladesh	Population and health IV	180.0	61.5
C	1992	AF	Niger	Population	17.6	11.6
C	1992	AF	Mauritania	Health and population	15.7	6.9
C	1992	AF	Equatorial Guinea	Health improvement	5.5	0.2
L	1992	EC	Poland	Health	130.0	6.5
L	1992	EC	Romania	Health services rehabilitation	150.0	14.4
C	1992	LA	Honduras	Social investment fund II	10.2	0.1
C	1992	LA	Guyana	Health, nutrition, and sanitation	10.3	0.2
C	1992	SA	India	Family welfare	79.0	63.2
C	1992	SA	India	Child survival and safe motherhood	214.5	0.1
C	1993	AF	Burundi	Social action	10.4	0.5
C	1993	AF	Guinea-Bissau	Social sector	8.8	0.9
C	1993	AF	Angola	First health	19.9	0.6
L	1993	EA	Papua New Guinea	Population and family planning	6.9	6.9

(Table continues on the following page)

Table B-1 *(continued)*

Loan/ credit	Fiscal year	Region[a]	Country	Project name	Lending amount (millions)	Amount for population programs (millions)
C	1993	EA	Philippines	Urban health and nutrition	70.0	17.5
L	1993	EA	Indonesia	Third community health and nutrition	93.5	9.4
C	1993	LA	Honduras	Nutrition and health	25.0	0.1
L	1993	LA	Ecuador	Second social development	70.0	15.4
L	1993	LA	Colombia	Municipal health	50.0	5.0
L	1993	LA	Guatemala	Social investment fund	20.0	0.6
C	1993	MN	Yemen	Family health V	26.6	10.7
L	1993	MN	Iran	Health and family planning	141.4	59.5
L	1993	MN	Jordan	Health management	20.0	2.0
C	1993	SA	India	Social safety nets	500.0	40.0
C	1993	SA	Pakistan	Second family health	48.0	12.0

a. AF, Africa; EA, East Asia and the Pacific; EC, Eastern and Central Europe; LA, Latin America and the Caribbean; MN, Middle East and North Africa; SA, South Asia.
Source: World Bank data.

Table B-2.   World Bank Lending for Population, by Region, 1970–93
(new commitments in millions of current U.S. dollars)

Fiscal year	Latin America and the Caribbean	Middle East and North Africa	East Asia and the Pacific	South Asia	Africa	Eastern and Central Europe	Total
1970	2.0	0.0	0.0	0.0	0.0	0.0	2.0
1971	3.0	4.8	0.0	0.0	0.0	0.0	7.8
1972	0.0	0.0	13.2	21.1	0.0	0.0	34.3
1973	0.0	0.0	5.0	0.0	0.0	0.0	5.0
1974	0.0	4.8	0.0	0.0	12.0	0.0	16.8
1975	0.0	0.0	25.0	15.0	0.0	0.0	40.0
1976	6.8	0.0	0.0	0.0	0.0	0.0	6.8
1977	5.0	0.0	24.5	0.0	0.0	0.0	29.5
1978	0.0	0.0	33.1	0.0	0.0	0.0	33.1
1979	0.0	25.0	57.0	32.0	0.0	0.0	114.0
1980	0.0	0.0	65.0	46.0	0.0	0.0	111.0
1981	0.0	1.1	0.0	0.0	0.0	0.0	1.1
1982	0.0	0.0	0.0	0.0	23.0	0.0	23.0
1983	1.0	0.0	0.0	18.0	2.0	0.0	21.0
1984	0.0	0.0	0.0	70.0	2.7	0.0	72.7
1985	0.0	6.2	46.0	0.0	2.6	0.0	54.8
1986	0.3	0.0	0.0	129.0	9.7	0.0	139.0
1987	6.8	0.0	0.0	0.0	7.9	0.0	14.7
1988	0.0	0.0	0.0	62.3	29.9	0.0	92.2
1989	0.0	0.4	0.0	124.6	0.4	0.0	125.4
1990	15.0	11.9	0.0	96.7	45.7	0.0	169.3
1991	10.7	26.0	104.0	75.0	135.3	0.0	351.0
1992	0.3	0.0	0.0	63.3	18.7	20.9	103.2
1993	21.1	72.2	33.8	52.0	2.0	0.0	181.1
Total	72.0	152.4	406.6	805.0	291.9	20.9	1,748.8

Source: For 1970–90, Sinding 1991, table A-1; for 1991–93, World Bank data.

limited to direct and indirect support of family planning service delivery, population policy development, and fertility survey/census work (see table B-1 for a list of Bank projects in fiscal 1970–93 that supported population activities).

Based on this strict definition, the key markers of the Bank's contribution to population are as follows: it has loaned more than $1.7 billion to support population activities over the past twenty-five years; the current (fiscal 1993) portfolio stands at $1.1 billion and new commitments for the fiscal 1990–93 period averaged $200 million a year (see table B-2 for a summary of lending statistics). The size of the portfolio has grown steadily, with the current portfolio representing more than 60 percent of all lending ever committed for population activities.

Findings of Major
Reviews of Bank Work
in Population

- External Advisory Panel on Population. 1976. "Report of the External Advisory Panel on Population [The Berelson Report]." Washington, D.C.

This report began with a review of population growth issues in developing countries, then addressed three sets of issues relating to the Bank's performance in population work.

The Bank's population policy within development. The review found that the Bank was not capitalizing on its main comparative advantage: its ability to strengthen demand for family planning through dialogue with government on the place of population in development and through encouragement of the socioeconomic conditions favoring fertility decline by way of greater attention to social sector lending and links. It could better integrate population into its own development activities through senior management statements of commitment; more social sector lending; systematic incorporation of population considerations in the Bank's economic analysis, "characterized as a major opportunity not sufficiently taken up"); and more research that is oriented to policy and operational issues.

The Bank's population projects. In this respect, the report was lukewarm. The Bank's assistance was marginal in comparison with that of other donors, the objectives of projects were overly ambitious, and the projects were expensive in terms of staff resources and impact, in part because of the Bank's mission approach. However, the review recognized the constraint on Bank assistance inherent in loans, not grants. Despite the difficulties, the report recommended continued lending operations, for the following reasons: Bank lending legitimized population activities as an appropriate area of government intervention, the record was not worse than in other "soft" sectors, and the Bank's lending for hardware complemented the activities of most other donors. More specifically, the report recommended broadening the scope of projects, particularly to include related health lending; being more innovative; examining procedures designed for "hardware" projects to ensure appropriateness for "softer" social sector operations; designing projects that support village-level involvement; considering sector loans; and emphasizing key countries defined according to level of socioeconomic development and commitment.

The Bank's population management. The report found attitudinal and organizational barriers to effective population work. Its recommendations were for increased training, increased donor coordination, more third-party participation in Bank ventures, closer relationships between Bank population departments and other appropriate Bank units, and the appointment of a special officer to oversee efforts to relate population to development activities.

- Barbara B. Crane and Jason L. Finkle. 1981. "Organizational Impediments to Development Assistance: The World Bank's Population Program." *World Politics* 33:4.

This report in a major development journal was a critical response to the Bank's decision to integrate population activities with health and nutrition. Its main criticisms were that the Bank had been slow to incorporate population considerations into its ongoing development dialogue with member countries, that its project loans had not proved to be an effective vehicle for strengthening national population programs, and that it had been unable to establish smooth and cooperative relations with other donor agencies in the population field. The authors acknowledged the difficulties of population operations but identified the chief problems as internal to the Bank: the resistance of its professional staff in other sectors, the lack of a strong base in the organizational structure of the Bank, subordination to other priorities (most notably health), and Bank project procedures. This unsolicited review was taken seriously by the Bank. Several of its recommendations—notably the development of a competent field staff and decentralization of operations, the offering of more sector loans, and the improvement of relations with other development assistance agencies—continue to receive attention.

- George Simmons and Rushikesh Maru. 1988. "The World Bank's Population Sector and Lending Review." Population and Human Resources Department Working Paper 94. World Bank, Washington, D.C.

The terms of reference for this next official external review were narrower than for the Berelson panel and focused on the Population, Health, and Nutrition Department's experience in project work and on the extent to which sector work had been instrumental in identifying and designing projects and fostering policy dialogue. The report identified lack of innovation in projects and the ways in which organizational procedures affected implementation and supervision as the greatest weaknesses in the Bank's population projects. It was also critical of the lack of evaluation built into project design and supervision. It recommended smaller, less complex projects; less reliance on ministries of health; and less emphasis on hardware, training, and management, and more on sustainability, on reaching the periphery, on information, education, and communication, and on evaluation. The review suggested that field staff would contribute to more effective implementation than supervision missions and urged greater coordination with other donors. The report also noted the constraint imposed by loans, not grants. The report found improvement in the quality and scope of sector reports but recommended more in-depth study of specific issues. The authors again identified attention to the links between population issues and development in policy dialogue as "perhaps the single most effective element in the Bank's work on population," although they found that the Bank had been more successful in this regard in smaller than in large countries and in countries with nascent rather than mature family planning programs.

- Population Crisis Committee. 1989. "The World Bank's Role in Global
  Population Efforts: An Agenda for Effective Action." Washington, D.C.
Produced by a population lobbying group, this report was strongly critical of the Bank's population work. It was particularly concerned about the effects of the 1987 reorganization on the Bank's institutional capacity for population, which it saw as fragmented by the organizational changes. It noted a wide gap between senior management statements on the importance of population and the lending program, which it criticized as deficient in volume, geographic coverage, and quality. It recommended changes in Bank incentives, organization, staffing, and project content. Several of the report's suggestions for change had Bank-wide implications, for example, the recommendation that the Bank provide grant assistance for population. Although the report voiced the concerns of many within the Bank, it was less optimistic than were Bank staff about the potential of the new Bank structure to generate new opportunities for lending.

- Steven W. Sinding. 1991. "Strengthening the Bank's Population Work in the

Nineties." Population and Human Resources Department Working Paper
802. World Bank, Washington, D.C.
This strategy paper, written by the Bank's population adviser, found improvement over the period of Bank involvement. Although the Bank's comparative
advantage in lending was found to be in infrastructure components, the most
successful projects were identified as those in which the Bank financed such
"software" and recurrent costs as training, transport, management information systems, and contraceptive supply. Projects that strengthened existing institutions were more successful than those that tried to bypass them by creating new ones. Where family planning was politically sensitive, Bank projects
were more successful where they sought to involve private and nongovernmental institutions. Lastly, the most successful programs included effective
monitoring and evaluation systems, and the Bank should be doing much more
in this area. In general, the report recommended, as did the Berelson report,
directing resources toward those countries where socioeconomic conditions
and the stage of program development indicated that government involvement
would be most effective. Like Simmons and Maru, Sinding found improved
sector work but insufficient attention to population issues in economic work
and policy dialogue. He noted the potential of the new structure of the Bank to
facilitate the incorporation of population issues into economic work and country strategy.

The report recommended stronger analysis of population issues in economic work, the development of population action plans where appropriate,
and consideration of population coordinators in each region; the granting of
high priority to training, population impact objectives, and evaluation in projects; and more use of resident advisers in the field. Over the long term, the
report recommended Bank leadership in resource mobilization and encouragement of consensus among donors that Bank loans should go to larger,
more mature population and family planning programs, freeing up grant funds
for newer programs that enjoy less political support.

● World Bank, Operations Evaluation Department. 1992. "Population and the
   World Bank: Implications from Eight Case Studies." Washington, D.C.
This review differs from the other evaluations of the Bank's population work
in that it is the only one based on detailed studies of experience. The report
concludes that overall, despite considerable diversity of activities and outcomes, and after slow and sometimes faulty starts, the Bank has become pro-
gressively more effective in the population field, although still more could
have been achieved. The report expresses concern, however, about family
planning being submerged in joint projects, about the growing size of projects

and sustainability, about neglect of monitoring and evaluation, and about the need to recognize the staff-intensive nature of population operations.

More broadly, in confirmation of the early Berelson report, the review finds that the Bank could have accomplished more by searching for selective interventions into the development process that had the potential for changing implicit benefits and costs of large families. It notes the obstacles to making this broader view operational: skepticism about the importance of demand-side interventions and staff compartmentalization and inertia. Nevertheless, it argues that population is not a discrete sector any more than economic development or poverty alleviation. All three are strategic objectives that should be the responsibility of all sectors. In the report's judgment, the new structure of the Bank provides the opportunity to support those interventions known to be associated with fertility decline. Strengthening the Bank's population work depends on forceful and consistent implementation of these recent changes.

References

Acsadi, George T. F., Gwendolyn Johnson-Acsadi, and Rodolfo Bulatao, eds. 1990. *Population Growth and Reproduction in Sub-Saharan Africa: Technical Analyses of Fertility and Its Consequences.* A World Bank Symposium. Washington, D.C.: World Bank.

Ahlburg, Dennis. 1994. "Population and Poverty." In Robert Cassen, ed., *Population and Development: Old Debates, New Conclusions.* U.S.–Third World Policy Perspectives 19. Washington, D.C.: Overseas Development Council and Transaction Books.

APAC (African Population Advisory Committee). 1993. "African Population Program: Status Report." World Bank, Africa Technical Department, Washington, D.C.

Bach-Baouab, Anwar. 1993. "Niger: WID Assessment." World Bank, Africa Region, Sahelian Department, Population and Human Resources Operations Division, Washington, D.C.

Birdsall, Nancy, and Richard Sabot. 1993. "Virtuous Circles: Human Capital, Growth, and Equity in East Asia." Background paper for *The East Asian Miracle.* World Bank, Policy Research Department, Washington, D.C.

Bongaarts, John. 1978. "A Framework for Analyzing the Proximate Determinants of Fertility." *Population and Development Review* 4:3, pp. 105–32.

———. 1994a. "Can the Growing Human Population Feed Itself?" *Scientific American* (March), pp. 36–42.

———. 1994b. "Population Policy Options in the Developing World." *Science* 263 (February 11), pp. 771–76.

Bongaarts, John, W. Parker Mauldin, and James F. Phillips. 1990. "The Demographic Impact of Family Planning Programs." *Studies in Family Planning* 21:6, pp. 299–310.

Bos, Eduard, My T. Vu, Ernest Massiah, and Rodolfo A. Bulatao. 1994. *World*

Population Projections, 1994–95 Edition: Estimates and Projections with Related Demographic Statistics. Baltimore, Md.: Johns Hopkins University Press.

Bulatao, Rudolfo, and Gail Richardson. 1993. "Fertility and Family Planning in Iran." World Bank, Europe, Middle East, and North Africa Region, Country Department II, Population and Human Resources Division, Washington, D.C.

Casterline, John B. 1991. "Integrating Health Risk Considerations and Fertility Preferences in Assessing the Demand for Family Planning in the Philippines." World Bank, Asia Region, Country Department II, Population and Human Resources Division, Washington, D.C.

Chen, Shaohua, Gaurav Datt, and Martin Ravallion. 1993. "Is Poverty Increasing in the Developing World?" Policy Research Working Paper Series 1146. World Bank, Washington, D.C.

Chomitz, Kenneth M., and Nancy Birdsall. 1991. "Incentives for Small Families: Concepts and Issues." Proceedings of the World Bank annual conference on development economics, 1990. World Bank, Washington, D.C.

Church, Cathleen A. 1989. "Lights! Camera! Action! Promoting Family Planning with RV, Video, and Film." *Population Reports* J:38.

Cleaver, Kevin M., and Götz A. Schreiber. 1993. "Reversing the Spiral: The Population, Agriculture, and Environment Nexus in Sub-Saharan Africa." World Bank, Africa Region, Washington, D.C.

Cleland, John. 1993. "Different Pathways to Demographic Transition." Paper presented at Population Summit, New Delhi, October.

Cleland, John, and W. Parker Mauldin. 1991. "The Promotion of Family Planning by Financial Payments: The Case of Bangladesh." *Studies in Family Planning* 22:1, pp. 1–18.

Cleland, John, and Christopher Wilson. 1987. "Demand Theories of the Fertility Transition: An Iconoclastic View." *Population Studies* 41:1.

Cleland, John, James F. Phillips, Sajeda Amin, and G. M. Kamal. 1994. *The Determinants of Reproductive Change in Bangladesh.* Washington, D.C.: World Bank.

Cochrane, Susan. 1979. *Fertility and Education: What Do We Really Know?* Baltimore, Md.: Johns Hopkins University Press.

Cochrane, Susan, and David K. Guilkey. 1992. "How Access to Contraception Affects Fertility and Contraceptive Use in Tunisia." Policy Research Working Paper 841. World Bank, Population, Health, and Nutrition Department, Washington, D.C.

Cochrane, Susan, and Thomas W. Merrick. 1994. "Family Planning and Health." World Bank, Population, Health, and Nutrition Department, Washington, D.C.

Colclough, Christopher. 1993. *Educating All the Children.* Oxford, Eng.: Clarendon Press.

Crane, Barbara B., and Jason L. Finkle. 1981. "Organizational Impediments to Development Assistance: The World Bank's Population Program." *World Politics* 33:4.

Dixon-Mueller, Ruth. 1993. *Population Policy and Women's Rights: Transforming Reproductive Choice.* Westport, Conn.: Praeger.

Dixon-Mueller, Ruth, and Adrienne Germain. 1992. "Stalking the Elusive 'Unmet Need' for Family Planning." *Studies in Family Planning* 23:5, pp. 325–28.

Dyson, Tim, and Mike Murphy. 1985. "The Onset of Fertility Transition." *Population and Development Review* 11:3, pp. 399–440.

External Advisory Panel on Population. 1976. "Report of the External Advisory Panel on Population [The Berelson Report]." Washington, D.C.

Fathalla, M. F. 1992. "Reproductive Health in the World: Two Decades of Progress and the Challenge Ahead." In *Reproductive Health: A Key to a Brighter Future. Biennial Report 1990–1991*. Geneva: World Health Organization.

Gertler, Paul J., and John W. Molyneaux. 1994. "How Economic Development and Family Planning Programs Combined to Reduce Indonesian Fertility." *Demography* 31:1, pp. 33–63.

Gilluly, Richard H., and Sidney H. Moore. 1986. "Radio: Spreading the Word on Family Planning." *Population Reports* J:32.

Grant, James P. 1994. *The State of the World's Children, 1994*. Oxford, Eng.: Oxford University Press for UNICEF.

Haub, Carl. 1992. *The U.N. Long-Range Population Projections: What They Tell Us*. Washington, D.C.: Population Reference Bureau, Inc.

Herz, Barbara, K. Subbarao, Masooma Habib, and Laura Raney. 1991. *Letting Girls Learn: Promising Approaches in Primary and Secondary Education*. Discussion Paper 133. Washington, D.C.: World Bank.

IPPF (International Planned Parenthood Federation). 1993. "Special Report: The Need for Quality Care." *Annual Report 1991–92*. London.

Jain, Anrudh. 1989. "Fertility Reduction and the Quality of Family Planning Services." *Studies in Family Planning* 20:1, pp. 1–16.

Jain, Anrudh, Judith Bruce, and Sushil Kumar. 1992. "Quality of Services, Programme Efforts, and Fertility Reduction." In James F. Phillips and John A. Ross, eds., *Family Planning Programmes and Fertility*. Oxford, Eng.: Clarendon Press.

Jarawan, E., and others. 1992. "Chad: Population, Health, and Nutrition Summary Report." World Bank, Africa Region, Sahelian Department, Population and Human Resources Operations Division, Washington, D.C.

Jejeebhoy, Shireen. 1992. "Women's Education, Fertility, and the Proximate Determinants of Fertility." UNFPA Expert Group Meeting on Population and Women, Gaborone.

Kelley, Allen C. 1994. "The Consequences of Rapid Population Growth on Human Resource Development: The Case of Education."

Kelley, Allen C., and Charles E. Nobbe. 1990. *Kenya at the Demographic Turning Point? Hypotheses and a Proposed Research Agenda*. Discussion Paper 107. Washington, D.C.: World Bank.

Kelley, Allen C., and Robert M. Schmidt. 1994. "Population and Income Change: Recent Evidence." World Bank Discussion Paper 249. Washington, D.C.

King, Elizabeth M., and H. Anne Hill, eds. 1993. *Women's Education in Developing Countries: Barriers, Benefits, and Policies*. Washington, D.C.: World Bank.

Lloyd, Cynthia B. 1993. "Investing in the Next Generation: The Implications of High Fertility at the Level of the Family." Population Council, New York.

Mauldin, W. Parker, and John A. Ross. 1991. "Family Planning Programs: Efforts and Results, 1982–89." *Studies in Family Planning* 22:6, pp. 350–67.

———. 1992. "Contraceptive Use and Commodity Costs in Developing Countries, 1990–2000." *International Family Planning Perspectives* 18:1, pp. 4–9.

Merrick, Thomas W., and Population Reference Bureau Staff. 1989. "World Population in Transition," Population Bulletin 41, no. 2.

Metra and Associates. 1992. *Bangladesh Contraceptive Prevalence Survey 1991: Key Findings*. Dhaka.

National Research Council, Working Group on the Health Consequences of Contraceptive Use and Controlled Fertility. 1989. "Contraception and Reproduction: Health Consequences for Women and Children in the Developing World." Washington, D.C.: National Academy Press.

National Research Council, Working Group on Population Growth and Economic Development. 1986. *Population Growth and Economic Development: Policy Questions*. Washington, D.C.: National Academy Press.

National Research Council, Working Group on Factors Affecting Contraceptive Use. 1993. *Factors Affecting Contraceptive Use in Sub-Saharan Africa*. Washington, D.C.: National Academy Press.

Phillips, James F., Main Bazle Hossain, Ruth Simmons, and Michael A. Koenig. 1993. "Worker-Client Exchanges and Contraceptive Use in Rural Bangladesh." *Studies in Family Planning* 24:6, pp. 329–42.

Phillips, James F., and John A. Ross, eds. 1992. *Family Planning Programmes and Fertility*, chap. 5. Oxford, Eng.: Clarendon Press.

Population Crisis Committee. 1989. "The World Bank's Role in Global Population Efforts: An Agenda for Effective Action." Washington, D.C.

Pritchett, Lant H. 1994. "Desired Fertility and the Impact of Population Policies." *Population and Development Review* 20:1, pp. 1–55.

Robey, Bryant, Shea O. Rutstein, and Leo Morris. 1992. "The Reproductive Revolution: New Survey Findings." *Population Reports* M:11.

Rosenzweig, Mark, and T. Paul Schultz. 1985. "The Demand for and Supply of Births: Fertility and Its Life-Cycle Consequences." *American Economic Review* 75, pp. 992–1015.

Ross, John A., and Stephen L. Isaacs. 1988. "Costs, Payments, and Incentives in Family Planning Programs: A Review for Developing Countries." *Studies in Family Planning* 19:5, pp. 270–83.

Russell, Sharon Stanton, and others. 1991. "New Directions in the Philippine Family Planning Program." World Bank, Asia Region, Country Department II, Population and Human Resources Division, Washington, D.C.

Sanderson, Warren C., and Jee-Peng Tan. 1993. "Population Issues in Asia." World Bank, Asia Technical Department, Washington, D.C.

Saxenian, Helen. 1991. "Brazil: Women's Reproductive Health." World Bank, Latin America and the Caribbean Regional Office, Country Department I, Population and Human Resources Operations Division, Washington, D.C.

Schultz, T. Paul. 1992. "Assessing Family Planning Cost-Effectiveness: Applicability of Individual Demand: Programme Supply Framework."

————. 1994. "Human Capital, Family Planning and Their Effect on Population Growth." *American Economic Review* 83 (2): 255–60.

Scribner, Susan. 1994. "Policies Affecting Fertility and Contraceptive Use: An Assessment of Twelve Sub-Saharan Countries." World Bank, Policy Research Department, Poverty and Human Resources Division, Washington, D.C.

Sen, Gita, Adrienne Germain, and Lincoln Chen. 1994. "Reconsidering Population Policy: Ethics, Development, and Strategies for Change." In *Editor's Introduction to Population Policies Reconsidered.* Boston, Mass.: Harvard School of Public Health, Harvard University Press.

Simmons, George B. 1992. "Supply and Demand, Not Supply vs. Demand: Appropriate Theory for the Study of Effects of Family Planning Programs on Fertility." In James F. Phillips and John A. Ross, eds., *Family Planning Programmes and Fertility,* chap. 4. Oxford, Eng.: Clarendon Press.

Simmons, George, and Rushikesh Maru. 1988. "The World Bank's Population Sector and Lending Review." Population and Human Resources Working Paper 94. World Bank, Washington, D.C.

Sinding, Steven W. 1993. "Getting to Replacement: Bridging the Gap between Individual Rights and Demographic Goals." In *Family Planning: Meeting Challenges, Promoting Choices: The Proceedings of the International Planned Parenthood Federation Family Planning Congress, New Delhi, October 1992,* chap. 4. New York: Parthenon Publishing Group.

————. 1991. "Strengthening the Bank's Population Work in the Nineties." Population and Human Resources Working Paper Series 802. World Bank, Washington, D.C.

Subbarao, Kalinidhi, and Laura Raney. 1993. "Social Gains from Female Education: A Cross-National Study." World Bank Discussion Paper 194. World Bank, Washington, D.C.

Sundström, Kajsa. 1993. "Abortion: A Reproductive Health Issue." World Bank, Population, Health, and Nutrition Department, Washington, D.C.

Tan, Jee-Peng, and Alain Mingat. 1992. *Education in Asia: A Comparative Study of Cost and Financing.* World Bank Regional and Sectoral Study. Washington, D.C.: World Bank.

Teitelbaum, Michael. 1989. "Strengthing the Bank's Population Work: Scope, Focus, and Incentive." Alfred P. Sloan Foundation, New York.

Tinker, Anne, and Marjorie A. Koblinsky. 1993. *Making Motherhood Safe.* World Bank Discussion Paper 202. World Bank, Washington, D.C.

Tinker, Anne, Patricia Daly, Cynthia Green, Helen Saxenian, Roma Lakshminarayanan, and Kirrin Gill. 1994. *Women's Health and Nutrition: Making a Difference.* World Bank Discussion Paper 256. Washington, D.C.

United Nations. 1993a. "Demographic Impact of AIDS in Fifteen African Countries." In *World Population Prospects, The 1992 Revision,* chap. 3. New York.

————. 1993b. *World Population Prospects, The 1992 Revision.* New York.

————. 1993c. *World Urbanization Prospects: The 1992 Revision.* New York.

————. 1994. "Draft Programme of Action of the International Conference on

Population and Development." United Nations Document A/CONF.171/PC/1. United Nations, New York.

———. Forthcoming. *Women's Education and Fertility Behavior: Recent Evidence from the Demographic and Health Survey.* New York.

UNFPA (United Nations Population Fund). 1993a. *Global Population Assistance Report, 1982–1991.* New York.

———. 1993b. "Report on Collaboration of the United Nations Population Fund with the World Bank and the Regional Development Banks." United Nations, Governing Council of the United Nations Development Program, fortieth session, New York.

———. 1994. "Note on the Resource Requirements for Population Programmes in the Years 1995–2015." United Nations Population Fund, Technical and Evaluation Division, New York.

USAID (United States Agency for International Development). 1989. "Moving into the Twenty-First Century: Principles for the Nineties." Office of Population, Family Planning Services Division, Washington, D.C.

van de Walle, Etienne. 1993. "Recent Trends in Marriage Ages." In Karen A. Foote and others, eds., *Demographic Change in Sub-Saharan Africa,* chap. 4. Washington, D.C.: National Academy Press.

van de Walle, Etienne, and Andrew D. Foster. 1990. *Fertility Decline in Africa: Assessment and Prospects.* World Bank Technical Paper 125. Washington, D.C.

Westoff, Charles F. 1992. "Age at Marriage, Age at First Birth, and Fertility in Africa." World Bank Technical Paper 169. Washington, D.C.

Wilkinson X., and others. 1993. "The Availability of Family Planning and Maternal and Child Health Services." Demographic and Health Surveys Comparative Studies 7. Columbia, Md.: Macro International Inc.

Winikoff, Beverly. 1987. "Family Planning and the Health of Women and Children." *Technology in Society* 9, pp. 415–38.

World Bank. 1984. *World Development Report 1984: Population Change and Economic Development.* New York: Oxford University Press.

———. 1986. *Population Growth and Policies in Sub-Saharan Africa.* World Bank Policy Study. Washington, D.C.

———. 1989. "Pakistan: Rapid Population Growth in Pakistan" Concerns and Consequences." World Bank, EMENA Regional Office, Washington, D.C.

———. 1990. *World Development Report 1990: Poverty.* New York: Oxford University Press.

———. 1991. *Assistance Strategies to Reduce Poverty.* World Bank Policy Paper. Washington, D.C.: World Bank.

———. 1992a. "Malawi: Population Sector Study." Southern Africa Department, African Regional Office, Washington, D.C.

———. 1992b. "Population and the World Bank: Implications from Eight Case Studies." Operations Evaluation Study. Washington, D.C.

———. 1992c. *World Development Report 1992: Development and the Environment.* New York: Oxford University Press.

———. 1993a. *The East Asian Miracle: Economic Growth and Public Policy.* New York: Oxford University Press.

———. 1993b. "Effective Family Planning Programs." Washington, D.C.

———. 1993c. *Poverty Reduction Handbook.* Washington, D.C.

———. 1993d. *Ukraine: The Social Sectors during Transition.* Washington, D.C.: World Bank.

———. 1993e. *World Development Report 1993: Investing in Health.* New York: Oxford University Press.

———. 1994a. *Averting the Old Age Crisis: How to Protect the Old and Promote Growth.* New York: Oxford University Press.

———. 1994b. *Enhancing Women's Participation in Economic Development.* Washington, D.C.

World Scientific Academies. 1993. *Population Summit of the World's Scientific Academies.* Washington, D.C.: National Academy Press.